BOND MARKET GUIDE FOR MONGOLIA

FEBRUARY 2021

ASIAN DEVELOPMENT BANK

ADB

© 2021 Asian Development Bank
6 ADB Avenue, Mandaluyong City, 1550 Metro Manila, Philippines
Tel +63 2 8632 4444; Fax +63 2 8636 2444
www.adb.org

Some rights reserved. Published in 2021.

ISBN 978-92-9262-727-0 (print); 978-92-9262-728-7 (electronic); 978-92-9262-729-4 (ebook)
Publication Stock No. SPR210065-2
DOI: http://dx.doi.org/10.22617/SPR210065-2

The views expressed in this publication are those of the authors and do not necessarily reflect the views and policies of the Asian Development Bank (ADB) or its Board of Governors or the governments they represent.

ADB does not guarantee the accuracy of the data included in this publication and accepts no responsibility for any consequence of their use. The mention of specific companies or products of manufacturers does not imply that they are endorsed or recommended by ADB in preference to others of a similar nature that are not mentioned.

By making any designation of or reference to a particular territory or geographic area, or by using the term "country" in this document, ADB does not intend to make any judgments as to the legal or other status of any territory or area.

Please contact pubsmarketing@adb.org if you have questions or comments with respect to content, or if you wish to obtain copyright permission for your intended use that does not fall within these terms, or for permission to use the ADB logo.

Corrigenda to ADB publications may be found at http://www.adb.org/publications/corrigenda.

Notes:
In this publication, "$" refers to United States dollars.
In this report, international standards for naming conventions—International Organization for Standardization (ISO) 3166 for country codes and ISO 4217 for currency codes—are used.

Printed on recycled paper

Contents

Contents

Tables and Figures

Foreword

As the Group of Twenty has stated, the development of local currency (LCY) bond markets plays an important role in diversifying financial intermediary channels and mitigating the impacts of financial crises on the real economy. This is all the more relevant in the context of the coronavirus disease, which had hit economies hard and squeezed finances. In addition, developed bond markets can support infrastructure finance, which is critical for emerging Asian economies to ensure further economic development.

Since 2002, the Asian Development Bank has been working closely with the Association of Southeast Asian Nations (ASEAN) and Japan, the People's Republic of China, and the Republic of Korea—collectively known as ASEAN+3—under the Asian Bond Markets Initiative (ABMI) to develop resilient regional financial systems. Mongolia became an official observer of ASEAN+3 Bond Market Forum in 2019 and has been an active participant since then.

This Bond Market Guide for Mongolia provides comprehensive information on the Mongolian LCY bond market. More importantly, through the process of drafting this publication, we can share our experiences and lessons learned with Mongolian authorities, key actors in maintaining market infrastructure, and market participants. We can also learn how Mongolia is trying to develop its market. Every market has its own unique features that make it impossible to apply a one-size-fits-all approach; thus, such close, market-specific dialogue is indispensable.

It is our hope that this Bond Market Guide for Mongolia will contribute to a better understanding of the LCY bond market and facilitate its further development.

James Patrick Lynch
Director General
East Asia Department

Acknowledgments

The Bond Market Guide for Mongolia was supported by the technical assistance for Macroeconomic Advisory Support for Mongolia. The project covered assistance in finalizing the Bond Market Guide for Mongolia with their strong support and contributions of the related parties from Mongolia.

The bond market guide drafting team—comprising Satoru Yamadera, principal financial sector specialist, Economic Research and Regional Cooperation Department (ERCD) of the Asian Development Bank (ADB); Kosintr Puongsophol, financial sector specialist, ERCD; and Bilguun "Bill" Dashdorj, ADB consultant—would like to thank Shigehito Inukai, former professor of Waseda University, Japan, and executive member of Capital Markets Association for Asia; Yoshiaki Wada, senior manager, NTT Data System Technologies, and chair of XBRL Asia Roundtable for their contribution; and Namuugerel Batbayar, ADB consultant. Also, the drafting team would like to thank Junkyu Lee, chief, Finance Sector Group, Sustainable Development and Climate Change Department, ADB and Donghyun Park, principal economist, ERCD for their kind peer review.

We would also like to express our special thanks to Zorigtbat Tseveenjav, director general of the Financial Policy Department, Ministry of Finance Mongolia (MOF); Sonor Luvsandorj, head of Financial Markets and Insurance Division, MOF; Undraa Nursed, analyst at the Financial Markets and Insurance Division, MOF; Amarbayasgalan Batbaatar, specialist at the Financial Markets and Insurance Division, MOF; Gerelmaa Bayarmagnai, economist at the Reserve Management and Financial Markets Department of the Bank of Mongolia; Tumurkhuyag Batsuuri, officer at the Securities Market Department of the Financial Regulatory Commission; Khuyag Tsedendamba, chief executive officer of the Mongolian Association of Securities Dealers; Mendjargal Orosoo, risk officer at the Settlement and Risk Management Department of Mongolian Securities Clearing & Settlement Co., Ltd; Batsuren Batsukh, chief of Depository at the Custodian and Registration of Ownership Right Department of the Mongolian Central Securities Depository; and Javkhlan Ivanov, senior specialist at the Market Development Department of the Mongolian Stock Exchange. These individuals representing policy bodies, regulatory authorities, and market institutions gave their time for market visit meetings and follow-up discussions. They have also reviewed and provided inputs on a draft of the Bond Market Guide for Mongolia over the course of this joint project.

Finally, this guide is dedicated to the memory of Lkhagvazaya Vasha, former analyst at the Financial Markets and Insurance Division, MOF, without whom this guide and its future updates would not have materialized.

No part of this report represents the official views or opinions of any institution that participated in this activity as a drafting committee. The ADB drafting team bears sole responsibility for the contents of this report.

February 2021

Abbreviations

ABMI	Asian Bond Markets Initiative	ISIN	International Securities Identification Number
ADB	Asian Development Bank	JSC	joint stock company
AML	anti-money laundering	LLC	limited liability company
APG	Asia/Pacific Group on Money Laundering	MASD	Mongolian Association of Securities Dealers
BEFI	business entity with foreign investment	MCSD	Mongolian Central Securities Depository
BENFI	business entity with no foreign investment	MNT	Mongolian togrog
BOM	Bank of Mongolia	MOF	Ministry of Finance
CBB	central bank bills	MSCH	Mongolian Securities Clearing House
CEO	Chief Executive Officer	MSE	Mongolian Stock Exchange
CFT	combating the financing of terrorism	MSX	Mongol Securities Exchange
CRA	credit rating agency	NBFI	non-banking financial institution
DVP	delivery versus payment	NDA	National Development Agency
EFF	Extended Fund Facility	OTC	over-the-counter
FATF	Financial Action Task Force	SPC	special purpose company
FDI	foreign direct investment	SRO	self-regulatory organization
FRC	Financial Regulatory Commission	USD	United States dollar (ISO code)
GDP	gross domestic product		
IFRS	International Financial Reporting Standards		
IMF	International Monetary Fund		
IOSCO	International Organization of Securities Commissions		
IPO	initial public offering		

USD1 = MNT2,733.52
MNT1 = USD0.00036583
      (BOM rate at end December 2019)

Overview

A.   Introduction

The development of the bond market in Mongolia accelerated over the past 5 years, with government bonds being the main driver of growth and increased interest in the market. Between 2015 and 2017, local currency (LCY) government bonds were issued to the public regularly through the Mongolian Stock Exchange (MSE). Government bonds were the most popular product on the MSE, and retail investor participation in the bond market (in terms of trading volume) increased 5 times for the primary market and almost 30 times for secondary market trading volume from 2015 to 2017.

The bond market in Mongolia features a number of debt instruments from both government and corporate issuers. Debt instruments may be publicly offered (referred to as open) or privately placed (referred to as closed). There are different types of debt instruments available, including government bonds, central bank bills, publicly offered corporate debt securities, and privately placed corporate debt instruments. Based on publicly available data, the total value of outstanding debt instruments in Mongolia was MNT6.1 trillion at the end of December 2019 (Table 1.1).

Table 1.1: Outstanding Value of Debt Instruments in Mongolia
(MNT billion)

	Outstanding Value (MNT billion)
Government bonds	1,435.0
Central bank bills	4,663.5
Publicly offered corporate debt securities	N.A.
Privately placed corporate debt instruments	N.A.
(Privately placed corporate debt securities registered with the MCSD)	N.A.
(Privately placed corporate debt instruments, other than corporate debt securities, not registered with the MCSD)	Not officially available[a]

MCSD = Mongolian Central Securities Depository, MNT = Mongolian togrog, N.A. = not available.
[a] According to the Financial Regulatory Commission, the total outstanding amount of privately placed debt instruments issued by non-banking financial institutions was MNT23.5 billion at the end of 2018.
Note: Data as of 31 December 2019.
Sources: Government of Mongolia; Ministry of Finance; Bank of Mongolia; Mongolian Stock Exchange; and Mongol Securities Exchange.

Under the current regulatory framework, there is no official definition of a corporate bond in Mongolia. Short-term financial instruments with less than a 1-year maturity are also referred to as corporate bonds. In many markets, bonds are normally referred to as securities or financial instruments if they have a maturity of more than 1 year, while securities or financial instruments with a maturity of less than 1 year are considered money market instruments. As such, there is no official concept of commercial paper in the Mongolian bond market, which typically has a maturity of less than 1 year and is considered a short-term money market instrument.

Also, in Mongolia, corporate bonds or corporate debt securities normally mean publicly offered securities registered at the central securities depository regulated by the Securities Market Law. Therefore, privately placed corporate debt instruments are unregulated and data on such debt instruments are not available.

Driven by increased investor interest in government bonds, the issuance of corporate bonds and debt instruments has grown significantly since the temporary halt of government bond issuance in October 2017. Corporate debt securities and debt instruments are mostly issued through private placements in Mongolia, with maturities of 3–18 months. Under the current regulatory framework, the process of public offering of debt securities follows the same process as public offering of equities; thus, it involves various regulatory approvals that make it very difficult to attain timely issuances. Corporate debt securities and instruments are generally collateralized or guaranteed by a third party. Uncollateralized or unguaranteed debt securities and instruments are not accepted by investors, as retail investors are the primary buyers of privately placed corporate debt instruments. The absence of professional investors is a challenge to developing a long-term bond market.

Under the Securities Market Law, a privately placed corporate debt instrument is not considered a security unless it is registered at the central securities depository. Typically, privately placed corporate debt instruments are issued via underwriters or directly to investors, including individual retail investors, in the form of corporate debt instrument purchase agreements. Most of these agreements are not registered at the central securities depository.

In addition, there is no mention of the term "bond" in the Securities Market Law. Although market participants understand the meaning of the term, the legal terminology for bonds are "debt securities." Moreover, there are no terms such as "short-term note," "commercial paper," and "short-term bill" in regulations. Future revisions to the relevant laws and regulations are expected to clarify and rectify the current lack of different terminologies.

Regulators and legislators are working to mitigate these factors by pushing regulatory reforms under long-term programs such as the Parliament-approved Sustainable Development Vision 2030 and Government of Mongolia-approved National Program to Develop the Financial Market until 2025.

These legislative reforms aim to remove the obstacles faced by corporate issuers to publicly offer corporate debt securities in the domestic market. In addition, these reforms are expected to introduce the necessary regulatory environment for currently unregulated privately placed corporate debt instruments. They will also contribute to investors' protection.

Though there are some unique characteristics in the Mongolian LCY bond market, it seems most of the basic necessary elements of a bond market's development are present. The upcoming revision of relevant regulations will further support the development of the Mongolian LCY bond market. Foreign investor interest in the bond market is increasing as well, with foreign institutional investors opening local offices in recent years.

B.   Mongolian Bond Market History and Development Milestones

1991–1995:   The MSE was established on 18 January 1991 through Decree No. 22 of the Government of Mongolia to develop the capital market and conduct privatization as part of the process to transform Mongolia's political and economic regime from communism to capitalism. The first primary market issuance took place on 7 February 1992. On 28 August 1995, secondary market trading took place for the first time.

The Securities Law, which would be replaced by the Securities Market Law in 2002, was approved by the Parliament on 26 September 1994, and the Securities Commission was established as part of the Central Bank of Mongolia.

1996–2000:   As per Decree No. 246, dated 26 September 1996, the Government of Mongolia approved the Regulation on Issuing and Settling Discounted Government Bonds for the purpose of financing seasonal shortages in the state's budget revenue. On 25 October 1996, the first government bond issuance took place with the participation of commercial banks, individuals, and corporates.

2001–2005:   On 8 June 2001, the first corporate debt securities were publicly offered through the MSE, which was 4 years earlier than the first initial public offering (IPO) (25 May 2005). Since then, a total of 14 corporate debt securities have been publicly offered on the MSE.

On 12 December 2002, the new Securities Market Law was approved by the Parliament and the 1994 Securities Law was abolished.

The Parliament saw the urgency to separate non-banking financial institutions (NBFIs) from the Central Bank of Mongolia's supervision and approved the Law on Legal Status of the Financial Regulatory Commission on 17 November 2005.

2006–2010:   On 25 January 2006, the Parliament approved the Charter of Financial Regulatory Commission (Decree No. 45) and established a regulatory commission to oversee all finance sectors except the banking sector.

2011–2015:   The Ministry of Finance (MOF) and the Bank of Mongolia (BOM) approved the Regulation on Issuance and Trading of Government Bonds on 25 October 2012 (Decree No. 217/A-161), invalidating previous government bond regulations and enabling the issuance of government bonds only through the central bank's trading system. On 21 May 2013, through a joint order of the Minister of Finance, the Governor of the Central Bank, and the Chair of the Financial Regulatory Commission (FRC), the Regulation on Secondary Market Trading of Government Securities was approved.

The Securities Market Law was approved on 24 May 2013 by the Parliament. Following the law's passage, MNT500.0 million worth of corporate debt securities were publicly offered through the MSE between 2013 and 2015.

On 26 November 2014, the government approved the Regulation on Issuance and Trading of Government Securities (Decree No. 371), allowing issuance of government bonds to the public through exchange issuance in addition to off-exchange issuance through the

BOM.[1] The first exchange issuance of government bonds was conducted through the MSE in November 2014. Government bonds were issued through the MSE consistently until October 2017, when the MOF temporarily ceased LCY government bonds issuance as part of the Extended Fund Facility (EFF) program of the International Monetary Fund (IMF).[2]

The Mongol Securities Exchange (MSX), a privately held securities exchange, was established in May 2015 and received its License to Trade and Settle in the Securities Market as per Financial Regulatory Commission Decree No. 312 on 3 July 2015.

2016–present: As part of the EFF program of the IMF, the government increased the personal income tax rate from zero to 10% on interest income earned from bank deposits, effective 1 April 2017. This resulted in a surge of demand for tax-free, high-interest government bonds and increased interest in the domestic capital market among retail investors. However, as part of the IMF program, LCY government bond issuance was temporarily halted by the MOF in October 2017.

In the absence of LCY government bond issuance, local investors started investing in the domestic corporate bonds market, including privately placed corporate debt instruments. On 29 June 2017, the largest ever publicly offered corporate debt instrument (MNT6.0 billion) was issued by the MSE-listed Suu Joint Stock Company. The Suu Bonds were also traded actively in the secondary market, with trading volume totaling MNT4.8 billion since the start of its secondary market trading.

C.   Mongolian Bond Market Overview

The Mongolian finance sector is dominated by commercial banks, which accounted for 94.2% of total funding in the banking sector in 2018, compared with 5.5% for NBFIs and only 0.3% by securities issuances (Table 1.2). Since 2014, in a bid to develop the domestic capital market, the government started issuing government bonds through the MSE. Prior to this, government bonds were issued and traded only on the interbank over-the-counter (OTC) market of the BOM.

---

[1]   Off-exchange issuance refers to the issuance of securities that are not listed on an exchange.
[2]   The IMF approved a 3-year arrangement under the Extended Fund Facility on 24 May 2017 to support Mongolia's economic reform program following a sharp decline in commodity prices and the slowdown in key export markets. The total $5.5 billion IMF-led financing package includes programs aimed at fiscal consolidation, to reduce the pressure on domestic financial markets, stabilize the external position, and restore debt sustainability, as well as to rehabilitate the banking system and strengthen the Bank of Mongolia, and a broad set of structural reforms, according to the IMF press release. The official press release can be found at https://www.imf.org/en/News/Articles/2017/05/24/17193-imf-executive-board-approves-financial-arrangement-for-mongolia.

Table 1.2: Finance Sector Financing in Mongolia

	2018 (MNT)	Percentage (%)
Bank loans	17,082.39 billion	94.2
NBFI and credit union loans	1,002.96 billion	5.5
Securities issuance	50.54 billion	0.3
Total	**18,135.89 billion**	**100.0**

MNT = Mongolian togrog, NBFI = non-banking financial institution.
Sources: Bank of Mongolia. 2018. Mongolia: *Loan Report of the Banks on December 2018*. Ulaanbaatar. https://www.mongolbank.mn/documents/statistic/loanbank/2018/m12.xls; Financial Regulatory Commission (FRC). 2018. Mongolia: *NBFIs Annual Report*. Ulaanbaatar. http://www.frc.mn/resource/frc/uploads/file/155124e5431fe6cedff390ed02ff681038745224.pdf; and FRC. 2018. Mongolia. *Credit Unions Annual Report*. Ulaanbaatar. http://www.frc.mn/resource/frc/uploads/file/ff4b41d932026709f704f729cfb1ca7d94175f93.pdf; Mongolian Stock Exchange. *Updated information of IPOs*. http://www.mse.mn/mn/content/list/116.

The domestic bond market's development accelerated from 2015 to 2017 as government bonds were issued to the public regularly through the MSE. Government bonds are tax exempt, making them attractive to domestic retail investors. Local companies can use exchange-traded government bonds as collateral for government tenders, which make them attractive for corporates as well. In addition, the government started collecting a 10% tax on interest income earned from bank deposits starting in April 2017; previously, there was no tax. These efforts drove increased interest in the bond market, with government bond trading accounting for 90% of the primary market and secondary market trading volume of the MSE from 2015 to 2017.

As public interest in the local bond market increased, corporate issuers started issuing corporate debt instruments in the domestic market as well. In 2015, after a 3-year absence, the first publicly offered corporate debt securities were issued on the MSE. In 2017, the largest public offering of corporate debt securities in the history of the Mongolian capital market was completed in the shortest period of time on the MSE. As a result, 2017 was the best year in the history of the MSE in terms of total primary market and secondary market trading volume, government bond trading volume, and corporate debt securities trading volume (Figure 1.1).

Figure 1.1: Primary and Secondary Market Trading Volume
(MNT billion)

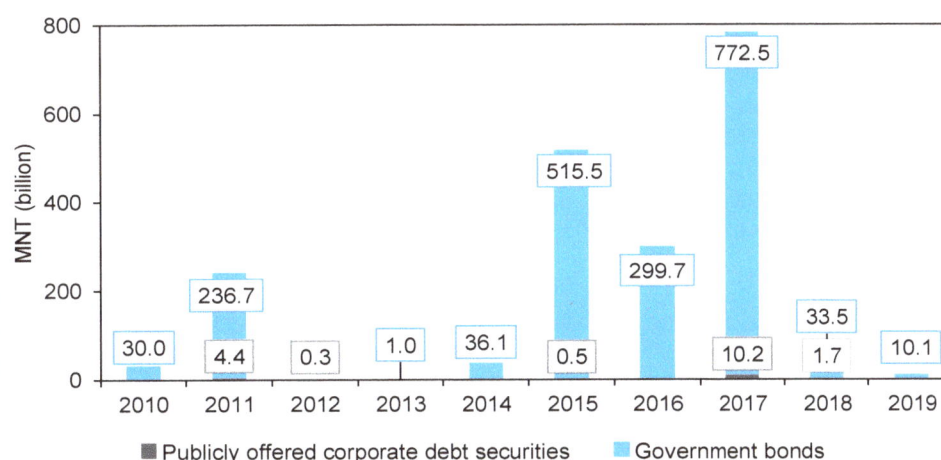

MNT = Mongolian togrog.
Note: Excludes the trading volumes of commercial banks.
Sources: Financial Regulatory Commission and Mongolian Securities Clearing House.

However, LCY government bond issuance was temporarily halted by the MOF in October 2017. As part of a USD5.5 billion multidonor financing package to support the government's Economic Recovery Plan, the IMF approved a 3-year arrangement for Mongolia under the EFF on 24 May 2017. The LCY government securities issuance was halted temporarily under the program to curb government budget expenditures, as these government securities had yields in the range of 12%–18% per annum.

In the absence of LCY government bond issuance, local investors started investing actively in the domestic corporate bond market, including privately placed corporate debt instruments. However, due to the fact that current regulatory requirements are the same for publicly offered debt securities and IPOs under the Securities Market Law and FRC regulations, public offers of corporate debt securities are required to go through a time-consuming and costly process for the issuer compared to private placements, which are unregulated. Since there have been no new publicly offered corporate debt securities issuances since June 2017 and no new government bond issuances since October 2017, the gap in demand for high-yield bonds is being filled by privately placed corporate debt instruments.

Because these privately placed corporate debt instruments are not regulated, there are no official data to gauge this market segment's development. However, one source of data would be the FRC statistics on NBFIs, which are regulated by the FRC and are one of the primary issuers of privately placed corporate debt instruments. According to the *Consolidated Financial Statements for Non-Banking Financial Institutions for 2018*, which is published by the FRC, the total outstanding amount of privately placed debt instruments issued by NBFIs were MNT23.5 billion in 2018, an increase of 241.4% from the previous year.

However, as the domestic corporate bond market's development is in the early stages, and with the lack of professional institutional investors in the market, retail investors are the primary participants in the market for privately placed corporate debt instruments. As a result, most of these privately placed corporate debt instruments have maturities of 3–18 months. In addition, there has been no unsecured corporate debt instruments issuance, as all of these corporate debt instruments are secured either by collateral or a guarantee from a third party.

D.   Challenges and Future Direction

Retail investors are the primary participants in the corporate bond market in Mongolia. Given the absence of professional long-term investors, the prevailing market practice when issuing corporate debt instruments in Mongolia is to guarantee repayment with collateral or third-party guarantees. This applies in both cases of privately placed debt instruments and publicly offered debt securities. Moreover, under the Securities Market Law, no distinction is made in requirements for debt instruments and other types of securities such as equities. As a result, the stringent requirements typically applied to public companies and IPOs are also applied to publicly offered debt securities.

In addition, there are not many legislations and regulations targeted specifically for the bond market. Current regulations require publicly offered securities to get approval from the FRC and the relevant exchange, and the securities prospectus required for public offering needs to include an audited financial report, legal opinion, and an asset valuation report prepared by a licensed valuation firm, which is a unique market feature in Mongolia that includes collateral or a third-party guarantee. These requirements intended for public companies during IPOs add to the cost and time required for publicly offering debt instruments in the Mongolian market.

To avoid the hassle and high cost of issuing publicly offered bonds, the current prevailing market practice for corporate debt instrument issuance is private placement in the form of loan agreements involving the issuer, the underwriter, and the investor. Privately placed corporate debt instruments are outside the scope of the Securities Market Law and are not considered as securities unless they are registered at a regulated securities depository entity.

The absence of a regulatory framework for corporate debt securities for private placements (placements for professional investors only), and specifically the lack of a framework for a professional-investors-only bond market that includes exemption from or relaxation of full disclosure requirements, is a source of major concern for regulators regarding the future development of the bond market in Mongolia.

Regulatory agencies are required to take measures to prevent gaps in regulation (vacuum lawless zones) to develop a healthy bond market and enhance investor protections. These efforts will contribute to fair price formation in the bond market.

The double-track development of two markets—an indirect financial market centered on banks and a direct capital market centered on the bond market—will increase the stability and sustainability of the overall financial market.

It is expected that these issues will be addressed in future amendments. Improvements to the regulatory environment are being planned under various long-term programs that will be described in the following section. Market participants and regulators are making efforts to prepare the necessary revisions to the relevant regulations as part of these programs.

E.   Roadmap for Developing the Bond Market

Legislators and regulators in Mongolia are implementing various long-term programs to aid the development of the Mongolian bond market and the capital market as a whole. The Parliament approved the Sustainable Development Vision 2030 on 5 February 2016, with the aim of increasing the capital market's share in the finance sector to 10% by 2020 and 16% by 2030, and decreasing the dominance of the banking sector to 90% by 2020 and 82% by 2030.

As part of the Sustainable Development Vision 2030, on 30 May 2019 the Parliament approved the General Directive on Developing the Economy and Society of Mongolia in 2020. Under the directive, the government will revise five pieces of legislation related to the capital market, with the aim of creating a legal environment to promote competition and accessibility in the finance sector, increasing product offerings, and streamlining regulations. These pieces of legislation include the Securities Market Law and Company Law, among others. The revisions are expected to remove some of the obstacles currently faced by corporate debt instrument issuers and poised to be completed in 2020 under the leadership of the MOF.

In addition, the Government of Mongolia approved the National Program to Develop the Financial Market until 2025 on 3 October 2017. Under the program, corporate and personal income taxes on interest income from publicly offered corporate debt instruments were lowered starting in January 2020. Regulators have also introduced delivery versus payment (DVP) settlement into the Mongolian capital market to upgrade the securities settlement system to meet international standards. The details of these programs are outlined in Chapter X of this bond market guide.

F.   Regional and Global Cooperation

There are currently no regional or global cooperative efforts with any countries or agencies outside of Mongolia with regard to the bond market. However, the MOF has joined the Association of Southeast Asian Nations and Japan, the People's Republic of China, and the Republic of Korea (ASEAN+3) Bond Market Forum under the Asian Bond Markets Initiative (ABMI) as an observer. The Asian Development Bank (ADB), which is the secretariat of ABMI, supports regional bond market development and shares the experiences of ABMI members.

II

Legal and Regulatory Framework

Mongolia's legal system is based on the civil law tradition. Most relevant laws and regulations for the securities market have been in place since the early 1990s when Mongolia transitioned from a planned economy to a market-driven one. Since the early 2010s, Mongolia has attracted increased interest in its mining sector from foreign investors. Significant revisions and additions have been made to capital market regulations since 2013 to attract more foreign investors into the domestic market and to keep up to date with global financial and capital markets.

A.   Legal Tradition

The legal system of Mongolia has changed since the democratic revolution of 1990 and is part of the civil law legal tradition.

B.   English Translation

1.   Translation of Legislation into English

Mongolia does not have an official requirement to translate legislation into English. Instead, the relevant regulatory authorities (BOM, FRC, and MOF) take it upon themselves to provide an unofficial English version of related laws and regulations.

As such, the unofficial translations provided by governmental bodies and regulatory authorities are practical resources for the study of the securities market. Some of these translations are done by well-known international legal firms and are chosen by the respective regulatory authority as a reference.

Although these unofficial translations typically state that every effort has been made to convey the meaning of the Mongolian version as accurately as possible, these English translations do not carry any legal authority. Only the original text has legal force and, hence, the English translation and the citations in the Bond Market Guide for Mongolia are strictly for reference only.

The most comprehensive list of respective laws and regulations in English can be found on the MSE's website; these translations are provided by an international legal firm with offices in Ulaanbaatar.[3] In addition, legislation related to the central bank can also be found in English on the BOM's website.[4] It is worth noting that some of the English translations may be based on an old version of the relevant legislation; user discretion is advised.

---

[3]   Mongolian Stock Exchange. Laws. http://mse.mn/en/content/list/167.
[4]   Central Bank of Mongolia. Legislation. https://www.mongolbank.mn/eng/listlawsandregulationsdb.aspx.

2.   Information Disclosure in English

There are no official requirements to translate or disclose corporate information in English or any other foreign language in Mongolia. As such, it is solely the discretion of the securities issuers and/or their underwriters to provide disclosure information in English in cases when the issuances are targeted to foreign investors.

In addition, official announcements and news releases by the regulatory authorities and the exchanges are not usually provided in English. Although some of these news releases can be found in English on the English versions of the FRC, BOM, and MSE websites, not all news is translated.

Issuers can translate disclosure information into English and have it announced through the English websites of regulators and the exchanges. However, although the regulators and the exchanges accept disclosure information in English, it does not replace the disclosure information required to be provided in Mongolian. Only the Mongolian disclosure information is accepted as official.

In the case of dual listing for a foreign-exchange-listed nonresident issuer, the disclosure information of foreign issuers is allowed to be in English, although the documents are required to be translated into Mongolian as well.

C.   Legislative Structure

Mongolia has a unicameral parliamentary system in which the President has a symbolic role and the government (Cabinet) exercises executive power. The legislative arm, the State Great Khural (Parliament), has one chamber that is chaired by the Speaker of the Parliament. The securities market is governed by a multitiered legislative and regulatory system structure.

The Constitution of Mongolia was enacted on 13 January 1992; put into force on 12 February; and amended in 1999, 2001, and 2019. Translated into English as the "General Law of the Mongolian State," it is the basis of the legislative and regulatory structure in Mongolia:

[1st tier] Constitution of Mongolia
  [2nd tier] Laws (key legislation issued by the Parliament)
  [3rd tier] Government resolutions and ordinances (issued by the Cabinet)
        [4th tier] Ministerial and regulatory orders and instructions (issued by ministers and regulatory bodies)
            [5th tier] Rules and guidelines of government agencies and institutions (issued by market institutions like MSE, MSX, Mongolian Central Securities Depository [MCSD], and Mongolian Securities Clearing House [MSCH] and approved by regulators).

International treaties ratified by Mongolia have equal weight as domestic laws except in cases when the application of an international treaty requires a new law to be in effect. According to the Constitution of Mongolia, international treaties and other legal documents that contradict the constitution should not be followed.

Table 2.1 lists the prevalent legislation and regulators for each of the individual tiers of the legislative structure of the securities market. Appendix 3 of this guide has the full list of laws, decrees, and other regulations directly related to the Mongolian bond market.

Table 2.1: Examples of Securities Market Legislation by Legislative Tier

Legislative Tier	Content or Significant Examples
Constitution	Political system, principles, rights, and duties
Laws (fundamental or key legislation)	• Company Law • Securities Market Law • Civil Law • Debt Management Law • Law on Legal Status of Financial Regulatory Commission • Investment Law • Asset-Backed Security Law • Investment Fund Law • Law on Settling Payments in National Currency • Law on Combating Money Laundering and Terrorism Financing
Government resolutions (providing detailed guidelines on implementation of the law)	• Government Resolution on Approving National Program to Develop Financial Market until 2025 (No. 299, 3 Oct 2017) • Government Resolution Regarding Regulation of Primary and Secondary Market Operations of Domestic Government Securities (No. 77, 20 Feb 2019)
Ministerial and regulatory orders and guidelines	• Ministerial Order on Approving Guidance of Calculating Price, Yield, Interest Rate, and Allocation of Domestic Government Securities Primary and Secondary Market, and Repurchase of Domestic Government Securities on Secondary Market (No. 280, 25 Dec 2019) • Ministerial Order on Approving Guidance of General Accounting Forms and Methodology for Business Entities (No. 100, 8 May 2018) • Financial Regulatory Commission Order on Approving Regulation on Procedure for Submission of Information and Monitoring of Stock Market Regulated Entities (No. 142, 4 Apr 2018) • Financial Regulatory Commission Order on Approving the Regulation on Information Transparency of Securities Issuers (No. 443, 17 Dec 2015) • Financial Regulatory Commission Order on Approving the Amendment and Revision of Regulation on Securities Registration (No. 408, 23 Nov 2015) • Financial Regulatory Commission Order on Approving the Regulation on Investment Management Activities and Permits, (No. 8, 15 Jan 2014) • Financial Regulatory Commission Order on Approving the Regulation on Regulating Financial Rating Operations (No. 529, 18 Dec 2013)
Rules and guidelines (of the MSE, MSX, MCSD, and MSCH)	• Mongolian Stock Exchange Board Order on Approving the Amendment and Revision of Trading Rules (No. 2017/08, 13 Dec 2017) • Mongolian Stock Exchange Board Order on Approving the Amendment and Revision of Securities Listing and Registration Rules (No. 2018/01, 25 Jan 2018) • Mongolian Stock Exchange Chief Executive Officer Order on Approving the Amendment and Revision of Guidelines on Primary Market Issuance of Government Securities (No. A/115, 4 Jul 2017) • Mongolian Stock Exchange Chief Executive Officer Order on Approving the Amendment and Revision of Guidelines on Trading Activities (No. 165, 17 Oct 2014) • Mongol Securities Exchange Board Order on Approving the Trading Rules (No. 14, 16 May 2018) • Mongol Securities Exchange Board Order on Approving the Listing Rules (No. 16, 24 May 2018) • Mongolian Central Securities Depository Board Order on Approving the Amendment and Revision of Securities Depository Rules (No. 7, 5 Jul 2016) • Mongolian Securities Clearing House Board Order on Approving the Amendment and Revision of Rules on Securities Clearing Activities (No. 6, 9 Aug 2016)

MCSD = Mongolian Central Securities Depository, MOF = Ministry of Finance, MSCH = Mongolian Securities Clearing House, MSE = Mongolian Stock Exchange, MSX = Mongol Securities Exchange.
Source: Adapted from the official websites of the Financial Regulatory Commission, MCSD, MOF, MSCH, MSE, and MSX.

1.   Fundamental Legislation

The fundamental legislation that establishes and regulates the main legal entities and their functions in the Mongolian securities market is the Company Law.

The Company Law (amended October 2011, effective November 2011) regulates the establishment, registration, and reorganization of a company; its shareholding and organizational structure; rights and obligations; and other related matters. According to the Company Law, a company may take one of the following two forms:

(i)   limited liability company (LLC); or
(ii) joint stock company (JSC).

An LLC is a company whose shareholders' capital is divided into shares, where the share ownership and rights are dictated by the company's charter and related laws. Although both individuals and companies can be a shareholder in an LLC, the maximum number of shareholders is limited to 50, according to the law.

A JSC may be either a public JSC (referred to as open) or a private JSC (referred to as closed). An open JSC is a company whose capital invested by the shareholders is divided into shares, which are listed on an exchange and may be freely traded by the public, as per the law. A closed JSC is a company whose capital invested by the shareholders is divided into shares, which are registered at the MSCH and MCSD, but they are not listed and traded outside of the exchange by means of private placements. Open JSCs are listed on the exchange and are required to report to the FRC on financial and corporate matters.

An investment fund is defined in the Company Law as a special purpose company (SPC) regulated by the Investment Fund Law (enacted 3 October 2013, effective 1 January 2014), and is not regulated by the Company Law. The Investment Fund Law defines an investment fund as a legal entity in the form of an SPC, although the specific definition of an SPC is not included in the legislation.

According to the Company Law, decisions to issue any security of the company, including debt securities, need to be made by its board (or shareholders if no board exists), unless otherwise stated in its company chapter.

There are no provisions in the Company Law in Mongolia related to the bondholders' meeting or bondholders' representative (or bondholders' agent or a bond-trustee-like function).

2.   Key Legislation

The key legislation that regulates the Mongolian bond market and the securities market at large are the Securities Market Law and the Investment Law.

a.   Securities Market Law

The Securities Market Law (amended in May 2013, effective January 2014) regulates the monitoring of activities of participants in the securities market and the protection of the rights and interests of investors.

The scope of the law covers securities issues, including corporate debt securities, by way of public offer, trading, and registration of securities; clearing, settlement, and deposit of securities; and other regulated activities in the securities market.

The law provides general regulation of the issue and trading of asset-backed securities. Detailed regulation of asset-backed securities is provided through the Asset-Backed Securities Market Law, enacted in January 2011.

Although a bond is defined in the law as a type of security, it is termed a "debt instrument" and there is no mention of the term "bond" in the law. Therefore, even though participants in the Mongolian capital market understand the term "bond," the legal terminology for bond is "debt instrument." Additionally, there are no terms such as short-term notes, commercial paper, or short-term bills in the regulations.

In addition, debt instruments are treated as a type of securities and no special distinction is made in the law, except when additional requirements are enforced when issuing them. Therefore, in addition to shares, all the necessary documentation and procedures required with regard to securities are also applied equally to debt instruments.

Shares and corporate bonds are financial products that are fundamentally different in nature. However, under the Securities Market Law, there is no way to distinguish them.

According to the Securities Market Law, securities may be issued for sale by way of public offer (referred to as open securities) or by private placement (referred to as closed securities). The public offer of debt securities is regulated by the FRC, while there are no specific clauses on privately placed debt securities in the law. A public offer means making an offer to the public, through news media channels, or the sale of securities to 50 or more persons in accordance with the procedures issued by the FRC, according to the law.

Although the law states that the FRC is the main regulatory body for public offers and the related procedures are left to the regulator to decide, the law lists certain requirements with regard to public offers, especially on the contents of a securities prospectus. According to Article 10 of the law, a securities prospectus is required to have the following reports from third-party professional institutions regulated by the FRC:

(i)   audited financial report by a licensed auditing firm;
(ii) legal opinion by a licensed legal firm; and
(iii) asset valuation report by a licensed valuation firm.

These requirements are enforced equally for all publicly offered securities, including corporate debt instruments. As such, preparatory work to publicly issue corporate debt securities requires significant time and resources from the issuer.

The securities prospectus and other required documentation is then sent to the exchange and the FRC, and it needs both their approval before it can be offered to the public.

With regard to the definition of an investor, the law does not specifically describe who is considered an investor, and it is only described as a securities market participant. However, the law defines professional investor (literal translation of the Mongolian version is "entity or person engaged in professional investment activity") as entities or persons engaged in a professional investment activity such as investment funds, pension funds, banks, and entities licensed to undertake activities related to NBFI activities, insurance, underwriting, or dealer activities, or other entities or persons considered as authorized to conduct professional investment activities by law or the FRC.

A professional investment activity is defined as investing in a professional and efficient manner with funds raised through an investment policy by entities specified in this law other than NBFIs, underwriters, or dealers. There is no differentiation between domestic and foreign investors in the law.

Even though the definition of a professional investor exists, a regulatory environment that focuses on the differences in risk-recognition and risk-tolerance abilities between professional investors and retail investors has not been realized. In addition, there is no market system for professional investors that allows corporates to issue securities with relaxed regulatory requirements and that can only be distributed and traded among professional investors.

Under the Securities Market Law, foreign-exchange-listed nonresident issuers can issue securities in the Mongolian market with the approval of the FRC. In such cases, it is not considered that the company is conducting business within Mongolian territory, according to the law. However, there is no specific clause on whether an entity registered in a foreign jurisdiction is allowed or not allowed to publicly offer its securities in the Mongolian market; there has been no such case to date.

b.   Investment Law

The Investment Law (effective November 2013) was passed by the Parliament in October 2013 to protect investor interests in Mongolia, especially those of foreign investors, and to promote foreign investment in the country. The purpose of the Investment Law is to protect the legitimate rights and interests of investors in Mongolia, establish a common legal guarantee for investment, support investment, stabilize the tax environment, determine the powers of state organizations and the rights and obligations of the investor, and regulate other relations concerning investment.

The law applies to both domestic and foreign investors and defines an investor in Mongolia as either domestic or foreign.

Investment incentives provided by the law are divided into tax and nontax incentives. Tax incentives include exemptions from taxes, tax credits, the use of accelerated depreciation for tax purposes, tax loss carryforward, and the deduction of employee training costs from taxable income. Nontax incentives include favorable conditions such as a longer period to possess land, incentives for conducting operations in free trade zones and technology and science parks, an increased quota of foreign employees, and simplified visa arrangements.

According to the Company Law and the Investment Law, incorporation in Mongolia can take the form of either a business entity with no foreign investment (BENFI) or a business entity with foreign investment (BEFI). A BEFI is defined as a company having shareholder capital of which not less than 25% is owned by foreign investors and each foreign investor's investment in the company is worth USD100,000 (or its equivalent in togrog) or more. There is no minimum amount of charter capital for a BENFI. A BENFI is converted into a BEFI at the point at which a foreign investor acquires 25% or more of the company's shares through sale, issuance, dividend, or otherwise. There is no special treatment of a BEFI over a BENFI in the law, as the objective of the law is to treat both foreign and domestic investors on equal terms.

3.   Legal Frameworks Specific to the Bond Market

a.   Government Bonds

As the development of the Mongolian bond market is in the early stage, there are not many pieces of legislation and regulations targeted specifically to the bond market. Debt securities are categorized in the same category as other securities under the Securities Market Law and all regulations regarding securities also apply to debt securities.

The most notable of the legal framework specific to the Mongolian government bond market is the Debt Management Law (enacted 18 February 2015) and the Government Resolution Regarding Regulation of Primary and Secondary Market Operations of Domestic Government Securities (No. 77, 20 February 2019), which regulates only government bond issuance procedures and government debt ceilings.

Before the temporary halt of government bond issuance in October 2017 under the IMF bailout program, government bond issuance and trading were regulated by the Government Resolution Regarding Regulation on Issuance and Trading of Government Securities (approved 26 November 2014, repealed and replaced on 20 February 2019). Under this previous regulation, government bonds were issued both through exchange and off-exchange, and the MOF could choose the venue of issuance. The off-exchange issuance was conducted through the BOM's interbank OTC market, while the exchange issuance was conducted through the MSE.[5]

The off-exchange issuance of Mongolian government bonds was only participated in by local banks through the BOM interbank OTC trading system, while the exchange issuance was open to other investors, including individual investors and banks, operating through brokers. To regulate government bond issuance, the MSE approved the Guidelines on Primary Market Issuance of Government Securities (amended 4 July 2017).

Because exchange issuance was termed "retail securities" in this previous regulation, the exchange-traded government bond market was called the "retail government bond market," while government bonds traded among local banks in the OTC market were called the "wholesale government bond market" in Mongolia. However, with the new Regulation on Primary and Secondary Market Operations of Domestic Government Securities, this terminology was removed from the regulation. The new regulation is yet to be applied in practice but will occur when government bond issuance restarts.

b.   Corporate Debt Instruments

For corporate debt securities, there are specific requirements for public offering of debt instruments in Article 16 of the Securities Market Law (amended in May 2013, effective January 2014). The Securities Market Law restricts the total value of publicly offered debt instruments to be not more than the value of its net assets or the sum of the value of its net assets and value of third-party guarantees.

In addition, the listing rules of an exchange have specific clauses regarding debt securities such as Section 14 of the MSE Securities Listing Rules (amended 25 January 2018) and Sections 15–19 of the MSX Listing Rules (approved 24 May 2018).

According to the MSE Listing Rules, the issuer for debt securities shall meet the criteria for MSE Board II listing requirements, which are a minimum of 2 years of operations and audited financial statements, net profit of no less than MNT100 million, or sufficient working capital to operate for more than 12 months. If the issuer does not

---

[5]   Exchange issuance means that the securities issued are listed on an exchange.

meet the criteria for MSE Board II listing requirements, then the issuer needs to be either fully guaranteed by the government or hold sufficient collateral assets to guarantee full repayment of the principal and interest payments, or the debt security needs to be insured by more than 80% of its total value. In addition, the listing rule requires that there shall be no restrictions on the free movement and trading of the debt securities, such as being locked for collateral pledge. For the MSX Listing Rules, there are no specific requirements for debt securities, except for a minimum 3 years of operation required from the issuer. (Listing rules are outlined in more detail in Section F of this chapter.)

D.   Mongolian Capital Market Regulatory Structure

The main regulatory body of the Mongolian capital market is the FRC. According to the Securities Market Law, the FRC is responsible for developing procedures, guidelines, regulations, and the approval of securities being offered publicly in the Mongolian capital market.

Before the FRC's establishment in 2006 with the Law on Legal Status of the Financial Regulatory Commission, the Securities Committee (now dissolved) of the BOM regulated the capital market. Although the BOM is no longer the regulating body of the capital market, it oversees the government bond interbank OTC market as the central bank and is the chief regulatory body for all issues affecting the banking industry.

On the other hand, the FRC regulates non-banking industries, including capital market participants, insurance companies, NBFIs, and savings and credit unions. Both the BOM and the FRC operate under, and thus report to, the Parliament. The charters of both entities are approved by the Parliament. The Governor of the BOM and the Commissioner of the FRC are also appointed by the Parliament.

The MOF plays a key role in legislation, regulation, development of the financial and capital markets, and the securities market at large. Government policies and legislation related to the capital market are generally handled by the MOF, and government ownership of the key agencies involved in the capital market is exercised through the MOF. In addition, the MOF is both an issuer and regulator of the LCY government bond market.

Prior to the temporary cessation of government bond issuance in October 2017, the MOF issued government bonds as per the Regulation on Issuance and Trading of Government Securities (approved 26 November 2014, repealed and replaced on 20 February 2019), which was approved under the Joint Decree of the Minister of Finance and the Governor of the Bank of Mongolia. Under this regulation, government bonds were issued through exchange and off-exchange methods. The off-exchange issuance was conducted through the BOM's interbank OTC market, while the exchange issuance was conducted through the MSE. Registration and transfer of ownership were made at the MCSD and the BOM handled the cash settlement process for government bonds.

The MSE, MCSD, and MSCH are fully government-owned entities, with ownership exercised by the MOF, although these entities are regulated by the FRC as per the Securities Market Law. The MSX, however, is a privately held exchange regulated by the FRC.

1.   Ministry of Finance

The MOF is part of the Cabinet of the Government of Mongolia (Figure 2.1).

The MOF is responsible for budget planning, monitoring government expenditure, formulating budget policies (including policies relating to debt management), taxation and customs, providing project financing, and monitoring the financial markets.

The main legislation on the roles and responsibilities of the MOF is the Law on the Government of Mongolia (enacted 6 May 1993) and the Law on the Legal Status of Ministries (enacted 15 April 2004).

The MOF is responsible for government bond issuance both internationally and domestically, and is both an issuer and regulator of LCY government bonds in the domestic market, under the Debt Management Law (enacted 18 February 2015).

In addition, the MOF exercises the government's ownership of many of the main capital market regulating entities (e.g., MSE, MCSD, and MSCH) and therefore plays an important role in the development of the domestic capital market.

Figure 2.1: Organizational Structure of the Ministry of Finance

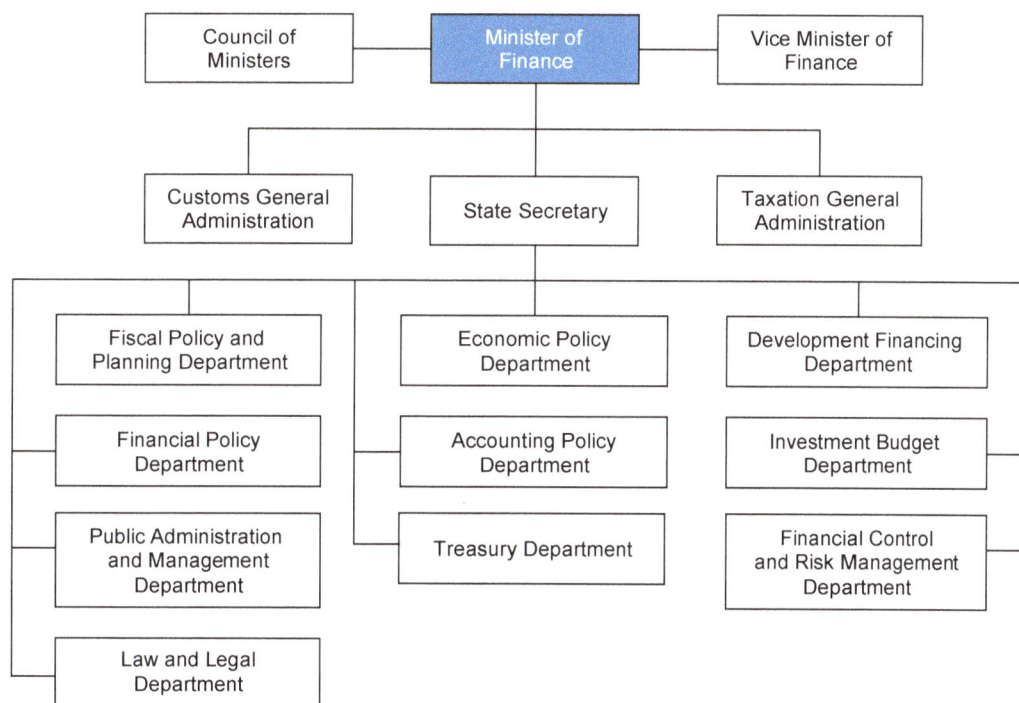

Source: Government of Mongolia, Ministry of Finance. https://mof.gov.mn/en/.

2.   Bank of Mongolia

The BOM was established in 1924. The main legislation setting the roles and responsibilities of the BOM is the Central Bank Law (enacted 3 September 1996).[6]

As defined in the Central Bank Law, the main objective of the BOM is to ensure stability of the national currency. As part of its main objective, the BOM is tasked to support the sustainable development of the economy through ensuring the stability of the banking system and financial markets.

As defined in the Central Bank Law, the BOM's primary functions are issuing and managing banknotes; formulating and implementing monetary policy; acting as a financial intermediary for the government; supervising the operations of commercial banks; managing, coordinating, and supervising the national payment system and its activities; holding and managing the state's foreign exchange reserves; protecting the rights and legal interests of bank customers and depositors; and implementing macroprudential policy.

The Monetary Policy Committee of the BOM is the central bank's monetary policy arm, which consists of the Governor, the First Deputy Governor, the Deputy Governor, and representatives from academia and the finance sector (Figure 2.2). The Governor, Director Generals of the Monetary Policy Department and the Reserve Management Department, and the Chief Economist decide the amount of liquidity absorbed from or injected into the interbank market on a weekly basis.

The BOM uses open market operations, which include central bank bills, repurchase transactions, swap and forward transactions, standing facilities (e.g., overnight deposits and up to 90-day repurchase agreements), and other instruments (e.g., reserve requirements and collateralized loans) to achieve its policy targets.

Under the previous Regulation on Issuance and Trading of Government Securities (2014), the off-exchange issuance of government bonds was conducted through the BOM's interbank OTC market trading system, and the cash settlement process was done through the BOM system.

With the newly approved Regulation on Primary and Secondary Market Operations of Domestic Government Securities (approved 20 February 2019), there is no longer a separation of exchange and off-exchange issuance of government bonds. The MOF is free to choose the issuing venue for public issuance and auction of government bonds, and the private placement of short-term government bonds is issued directly to the BOM. However, the new regulation is yet to be applied in practice and will be implemented when government bond issuance restarts.

---

[6]   As part of the IMF's EFF approved on 24 May 2017, the Central Bank Law was revised on 31 May 2017 and again on 12 January 2018 to prevent quasi-fiscal spending by the government. In addition, a key part of the EFF is to create a strong, resilient banking sector. The BOM is undertaking various measures such as asset quality review and the recapitalization of local banks.

Figure 2.2: Organizational Structure of the Bank of Mongolia

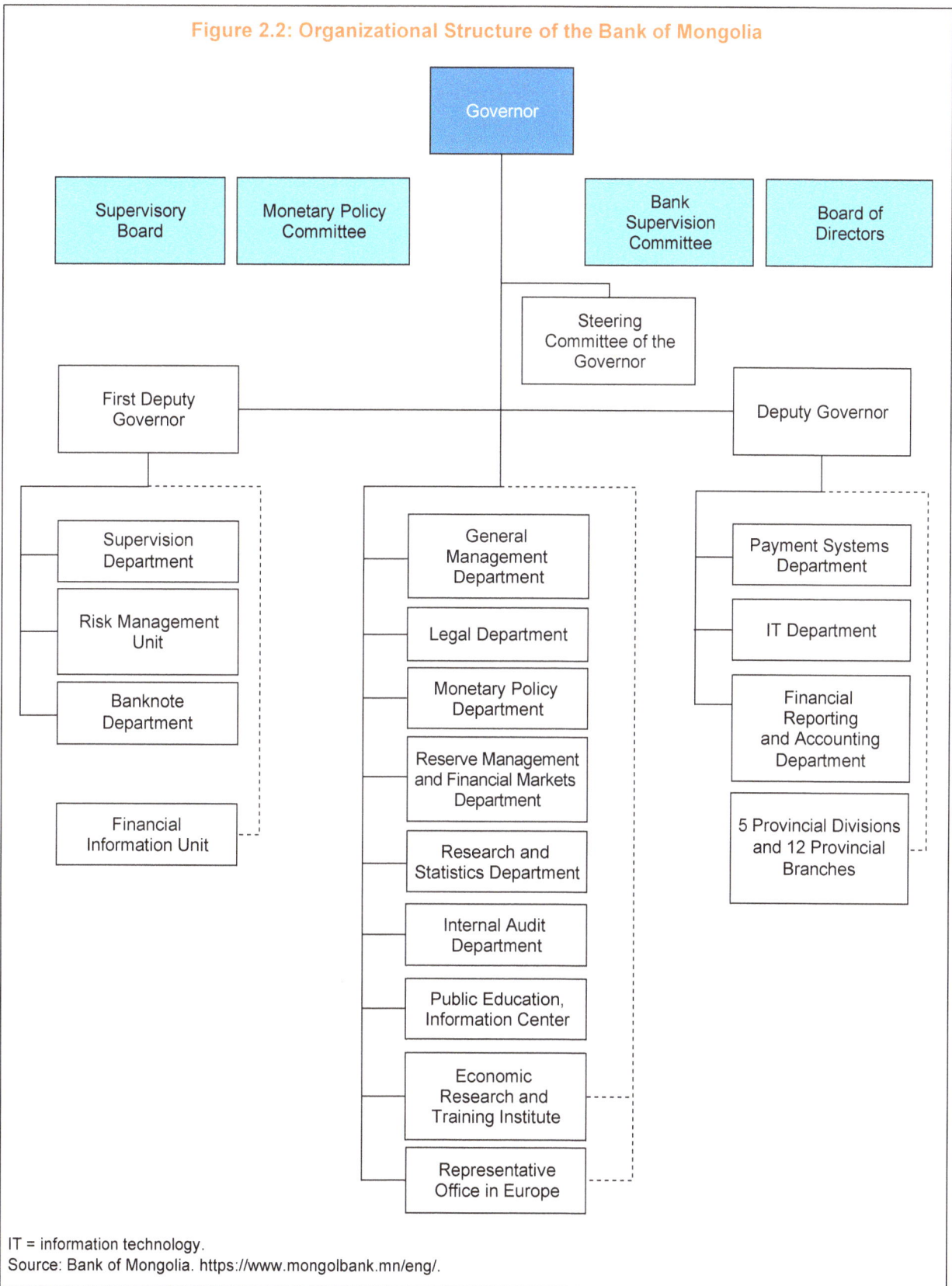

Governor

Supervisory Board

Monetary Policy Committee

Bank Supervision Committee

Board of Directors

Steering Committee of the Governor

First Deputy Governor

Deputy Governor

Supervision Department

Risk Management Unit

Banknote Department

Financial Information Unit

General Management Department

Legal Department

Monetary Policy Department

Reserve Management and Financial Markets Department

Research and Statistics Department

Internal Audit Department

Public Education, Information Center

Economic Research and Training Institute

Representative Office in Europe

Payment Systems Department

IT Department

Financial Reporting and Accounting Department

5 Provincial Divisions and 12 Provincial Branches

IT = information technology.
Source: Bank of Mongolia. https://www.mongolbank.mn/eng/.

3.   Financial Regulatory Commission

The FRC was established in 2006 pursuant to the Law of Mongolia on the Legal Status of the Financial Regulatory Commission (enacted 17 November 2005). Formerly, the Securities Committee (now dissolved) of the BOM had regulated the capital market since 1994 under the previous Securities Law.

The FRC was established to oversee and regulate the non-banking sector, including the securities market, insurance companies, NBFIs, and savings and credit unions, with its key goal being to ensure domestic financial market stability. Its functions include developing and implementing regulations to ensure the stabilization and regulation of the securities markets, supervising compliance with the relevant legislation, granting and monitoring licenses to carry out activities in the securities market, and supervising and training market participants. The Chair and the Commissioners of the FRC are appointed by the Parliament (Figure 2.3).

According to the Securities Market Law, the FRC is responsible for developing procedures, guidelines, regulations, and approvals of securities being offered publicly in the Mongolian capital market. Securities offered privately (referred to as closed) are not regulated by the FRC, and closed corporate debt instruments (privately placed corporate debt instruments) are not regulated under the current regulations.

Under the Securities Market Law, the FRC is tasked with regulating the following financial services:

(i)   activities of NBFIs;
(ii)   activities of professional service providers in the securities market, including listing authority function for exchanges;
(iii)   insurance activities;
(iv)   insurance brokerage and assessment activities;
(v)   credit union savings and lending activities;
(vi)   asset-backed security issuance activities;
(vii)   activities stipulated in the Loan Guarantee Fund Law;
(viii) insurance activities stipulated in the Index-Based Livestock Insurance Law;
(ix)   commodities exchange activities;
(x)   real estate brokerage activities; and
(xi)   other financial activities as defined in the law.

In the context of the bond market, the FRC approves applications for the issuance and listing of debt securities via public offering, and regulates and monitors securities market participants. The FRC also approves exchange rules and regulations prior to publication.

Figure 2.3: Organizational Structure of the Financial Regulatory Commission

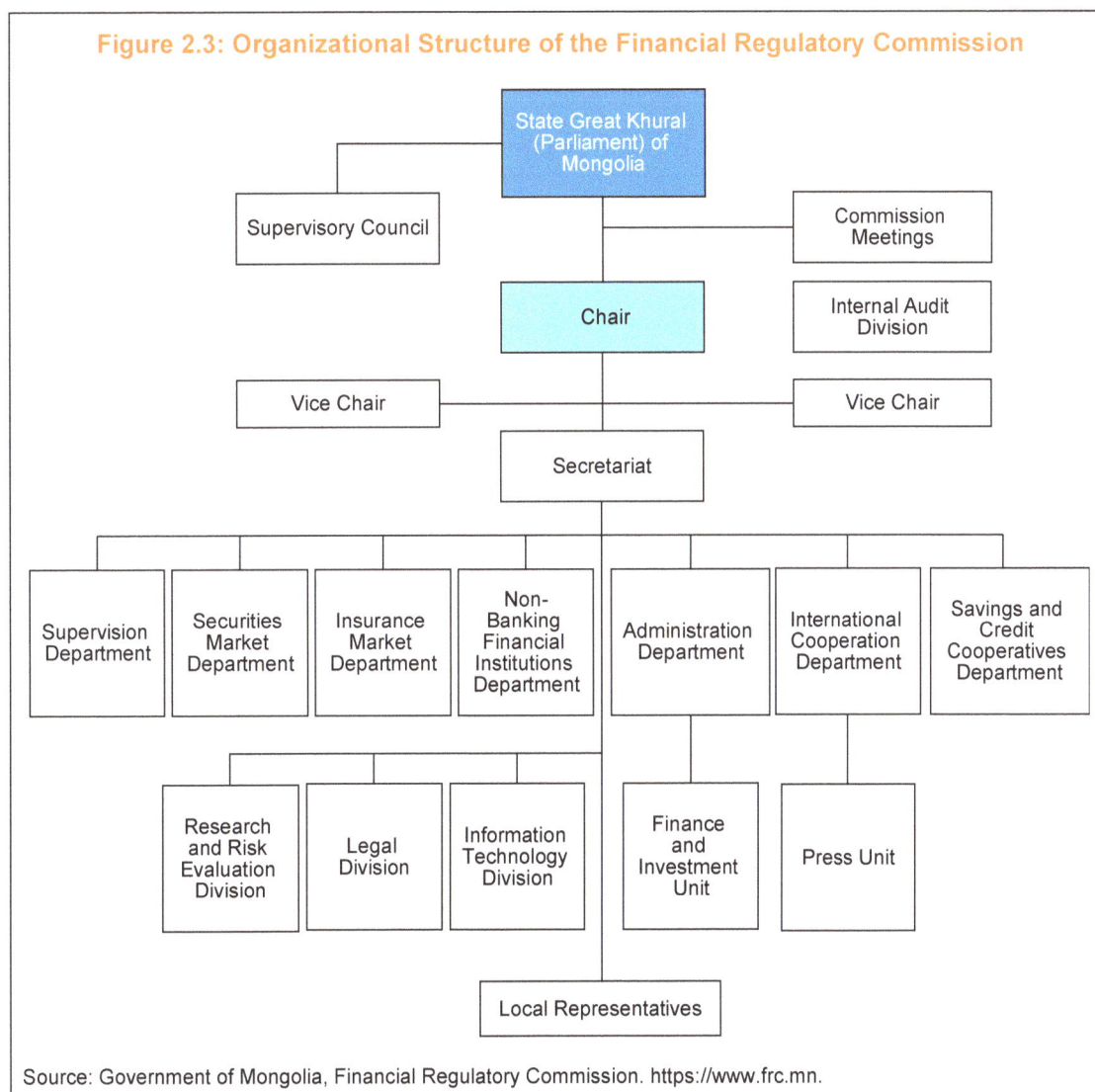

Source: Government of Mongolia, Financial Regulatory Commission. https://www.frc.mn.

4.   Mongolian Stock Exchange

The MSE was established in 1991, shortly after Mongolia's transition to a free market economy, to facilitate the privatization of state assets.

The main duties of the MSE include listing securities, organizing securities trading, enrolling securities firms as members, monitoring member operations, fostering capital market development, introducing new investment products and services, promoting information transparency, and improving financial literacy among the public.

The MSE is a 100% state-owned enterprise, with the MOF exercising the ownership rights of the government (Figure 2.4). As such, the management of the MSE is appointed by and reports to the MOF. The MSE is also regulated by the FRC, under the Securities Market Law, as a market participant with special licenses to organize securities trading granted by the FRC. As a self-regulatory organization (SRO), the fundamental purpose of the MSE is protecting its members' interests, establishing common procedures for professional activities and codes of conduct, increasing the capabilities of its members, and developing and ensuring stability within the securities market.

Listing corporate debt instruments on the MSE is effectively synonymous with approving issuance of the corporate debt instruments and allowing them to trade on an exchange. Listing authority function is held by the FRC, and the concept of profile listing does not exist in Mongolia yet.[7] For publicly offered corporate debt instruments listing, the issuer for debt securities shall meet the Criteria for Board II listing stated in Article 12 of the MSE Listing Rules (Chapter II.C.3 and F.3 has the details).

As of December 2019, there were 198 listed public companies with a combined market capitalization of MNT2.7 trillion and 11 LCY government bonds worth MNT34.2 billion, with maturities of 3 and 5 years, listed on the MSE. There have been no corporate debt securities listed on the MSE since June 2017. There were 52 securities firms with trading membership at the MSE as of December 2019.

In relation to the bond market, the MSE facilitates the public issuance and trading of securities, including publicly listed corporate debt securities. In addition, under the previous Regulation on Issuance and Trading of Government Securities (2014), government bonds were issued through an exchange and off-exchange; exchange issuance was conducted through the MSE between 2015 and 2017.

With the new Regulation on Primary and Secondary Market Operations of Domestic Government Securities (effective 20 February 2019) approved by the government, the MOF chooses the issuing venue for public issuance and auction of government bonds. Because LCY government bond issuance has been on hold since the 2017 IMF agreement, and the new 2019 regulation on government bonds has yet to be implemented, it is unclear whether the government will continue to issue government bonds through the MSE.

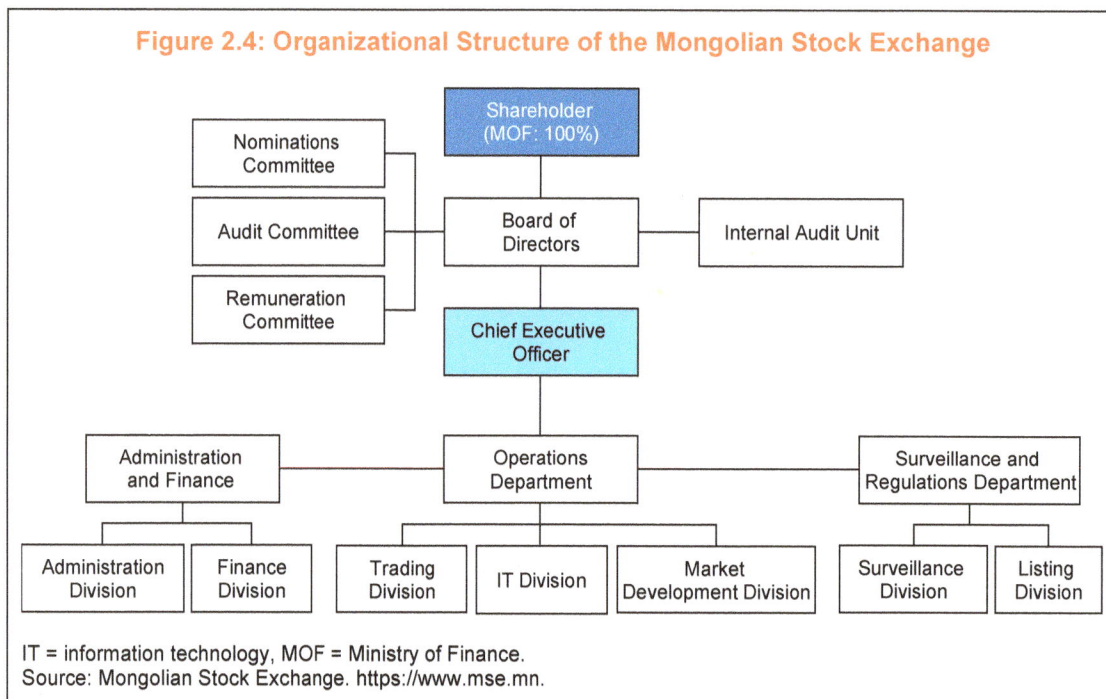

Figure 2.4: Organizational Structure of the Mongolian Stock Exchange

IT = information technology, MOF = Ministry of Finance.
Source: Mongolian Stock Exchange. https://www.mse.mn.

---

[7] A profile listing is a listing without trading on an exchange. The objective of the listing is to make debt instruments visible and more information available to investors via a recognized listing place, particularly those investors with more restrictive mandates, such as mutual and pension funds. A profile listing at a designated listing place can ensure the flow of continuous disclosure information and possibly even reference pricing in some markets.

5.   Mongol Securities Exchange

The MSX, a privately held securities exchange, was established in May 2015 and received its license to operate a regulated exchange in the securities market as per Financial Regulatory Commission Decree No. 312 on 3 July 2015 (Figure 2.5).

The MSX has license to undertake securities trading, as well as securities clearing, which are regulated activities under the Securities Market Law. The trading system of the MSX is provided by Nasdaq, Inc. It had 14 securities firms as trading members as of 2019.

As the new (second) securities exchange in Mongolia, the MSX had its first listing on November 2017. As of December 2019, the MSX had one company listed, with market capitalization of MNT2.5 billion, and one publicly offered corporate debt securities listed.

Due to the MSX having a license to undertake securities clearing operations, some of the more recent private placements of corporate debt instruments are using the exchange not as a listing place but as the clearing agent. In 2019, there were three instances of off-exchange issuance of corporate debt instruments issued using the MSX clearing system.[8]

Figure 2.5: Organizational Structure of the Mongol Securities Exchange

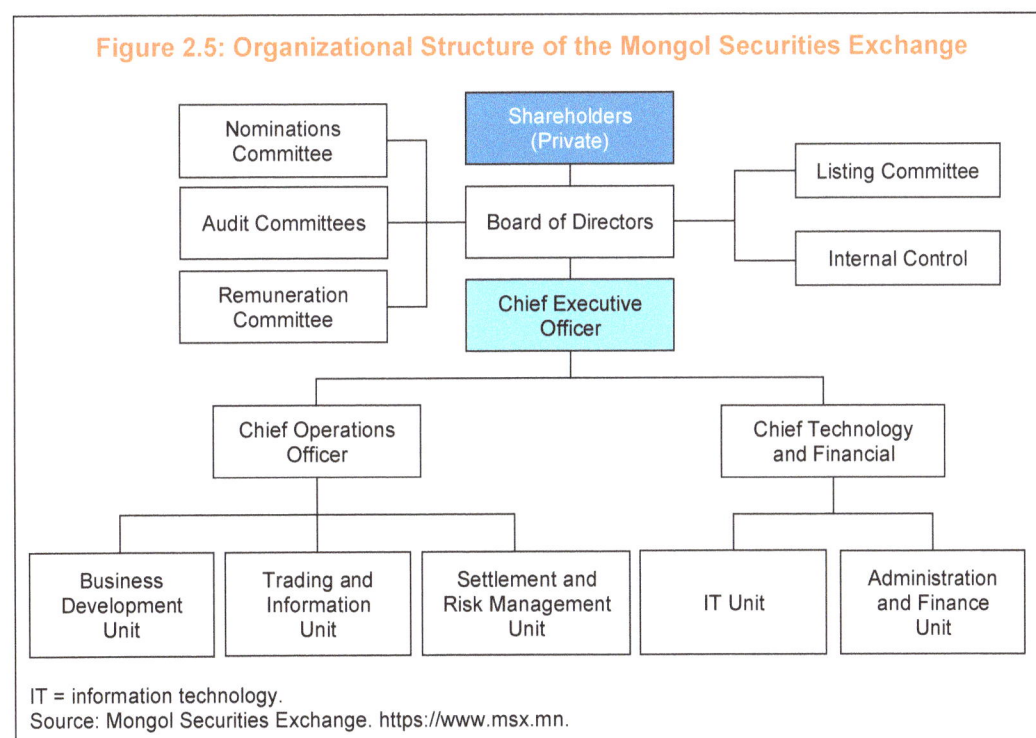

IT = information technology.
Source: Mongol Securities Exchange. https://www.msx.mn.

---

[8]   Off-exchange issuance in this case means the corporate debt instruments issued are not listed on the exchange and instead are privately placed.

6.   Mongolian Central Securities Depository

Prior to its incorporation, the MCSD was part of the Settlement and Depository Division of the MSE. As per Government Resolution No. 72 in 2003, the Mongolian Securities Clearing House and Central Depository LLC was established under the MOF to conduct registration of securities ownership rights, securities central depository, and securities clearing and settlement. However, in April 2016, the Securities Clearing and Settlement Department was separated as an independent company, the Mongolian Securities Clearing House LLC, and registration of ownership rights and the central depository department was reorganized as the Mongolian Central Securities Depository LLC, both of which are owned 100% by the government.

The MCSD operates with the following special licenses granted by the FRC under the Securities Market Law:

(i)   securities ownership rights registration services;
(ii)   central depository of securities; and
(iii)   custodial services.

The MCSD is 100% state-owned and, as such, management of the MCSD is appointed by the MOF and reports to the MOF (Figure 2.6). The MCSD is regulated by the FRC as a market participant with special licenses under the Securities Market Law.

In the context of the bond market, the MCSD conducts registration and depository services for LCY government bonds, as per both previous and new government regulations on government bond issuance, as well as publicly offered corporate debt securities, as per the Securities Market Law. In the case of government bonds, both exchange issuances and off-exchange issuances are registered and deposited at the MCSD.

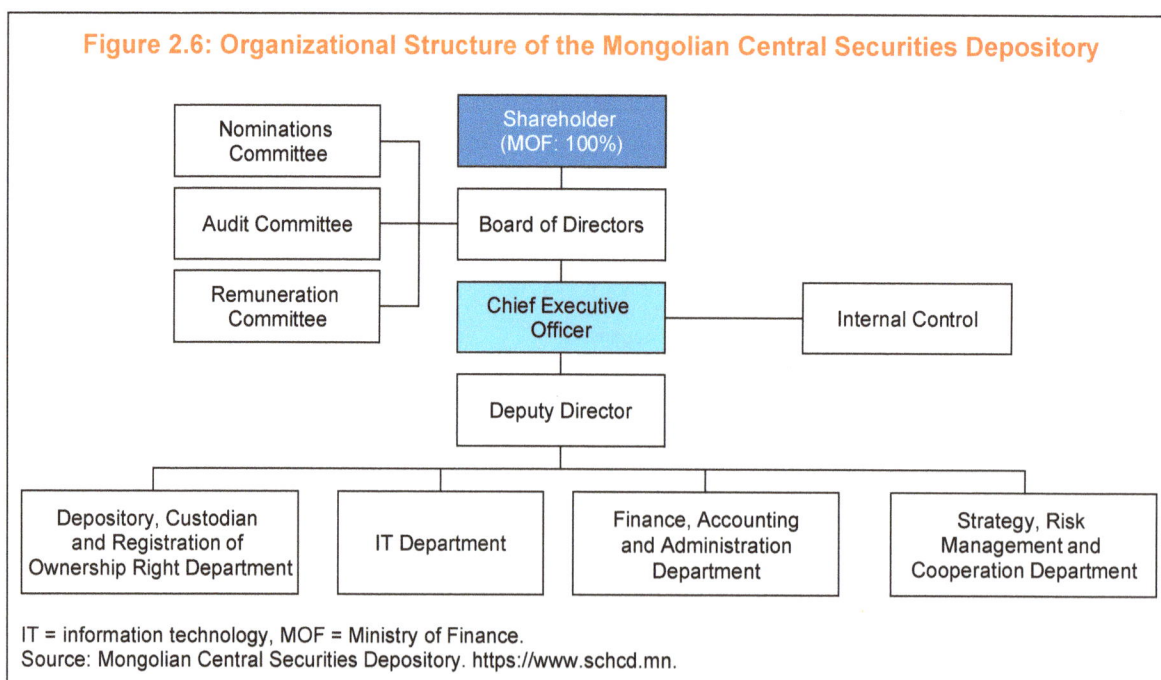

Figure 2.6: Organizational Structure of the Mongolian Central Securities Depository

IT = information technology, MOF = Ministry of Finance.
Source: Mongolian Central Securities Depository. https://www.schcd.mn.

7. Mongolian Securities Clearing House

The MSCH was established as an independent clearing and settlement institution in 2016 as per Government Resolution No. 147 on the Reorganization of the Central Securities Depository and Clearing and Settlement Company. Prior to that, it was part of the Mongolian Securities Clearing House and Central Depository LLC, established under the MOF.

The MSCH is 100% state-owned and, as such, management of the MSCH is appointed by and reports to the MOF (Figure 2.7). The MSCH is regulated by the FRC as a market participant with special licenses under the Securities Market Law.

The MSCH operates with the following special licenses granted by the FRC to undertake regulated activities defined in the Securities Market Law:

  (i)   securities trading related clearing; and
  (ii) securities trading related settlement.

The MSCH conducts securities trading related clearing and settlement via the real-time gross settlement system of the BOM. Because the MSCH uses the settlement system of the BOM, it is only responsible for settlement of publicly offered corporate debt securities and not LCY government bonds. Government bond cash settlements are handled at the BOM directly under the Regulation on Issuance and Trading of Government Debt Securities (2014). In the context of government bond issuance, the MSCH is a sub-participant and is not supervised by the BOM.

In relation to the bond market, the MSCH handles clearing and settlement of publicly offered corporate debt securities at the MSE. Because the MSX has a license to conduct securities trading related clearing, corporate debt securities clearing at the MSX does not go through the MSCH.

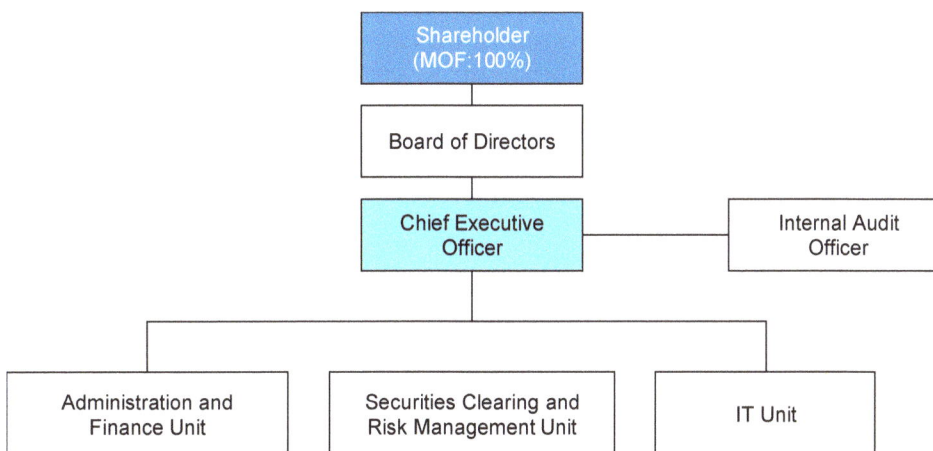

Figure 2.7: Organizational Structure of the Mongolian Securities Clearing House

IT = information technology, MOF = Ministry of Finance.
Source: Mongolian Securities Clearing House. https://www.schcd.mn.

8.   Mongolian Association of Securities Dealers

The Mongolian Association of Securities Dealers (MASD) was established in July 1995 under the mutual initiative of domestic securities firms. It is a nongovernmental organization with members consisting of market participants. The mission of the organization is to protect the common rights of investors and member firms; set ethical standards of professional conduct; create fair, transparent, and open markets; and maintain the sustainable growth of the capital market.

On 10 June 2015, the MASD received its status as an SRO under the Securities Market Law and is registered and monitored by the FRC.

As per its charter, the main duties of the MASD include the following:

(i)   organize trainings and certify market participants to conduct professional activities in the capital market;
(ii) formulate its own charters and regulations, and enforce member firms to abide by the rules;
(iii) set ethical standards of professional conduct and enforce member firms to abide by the rules;
(iv) conduct capital market research and analysis, and represent the capital market;
(v)   support active cooperation among capital market participants; and
(vi) cooperate with relevant parties to enhance the regulatory environment of the capital market.

The Ikh Khural (General Assembly) of the MASD convenes during the first quarter of each year. The Board of Directors can decide to convene an irregular assembly. The Board of Directors has 11 members, and the Chair of the Board of Directors is selected from among the board members by receiving equal to or more than one-half of the total votes cast. The Chair does not have tenure. The Secretary General oversees the daily operations of the MASD (Figure 2.8).

In the context of the bond market, the MASD is the main organization responsible for issuing professional certification for employees of market participants. In addition, in light of the emerging market for privately placed (closed) corporate debt instruments, the MASD is actively participating in regulating and monitoring this new market by drafting new regulations for the OTC market. The draft regulation on the OTC market is yet to be ratified by the FRC. There were no regulations for the OTC market in Mongolia at the time of writing this bond market guide.

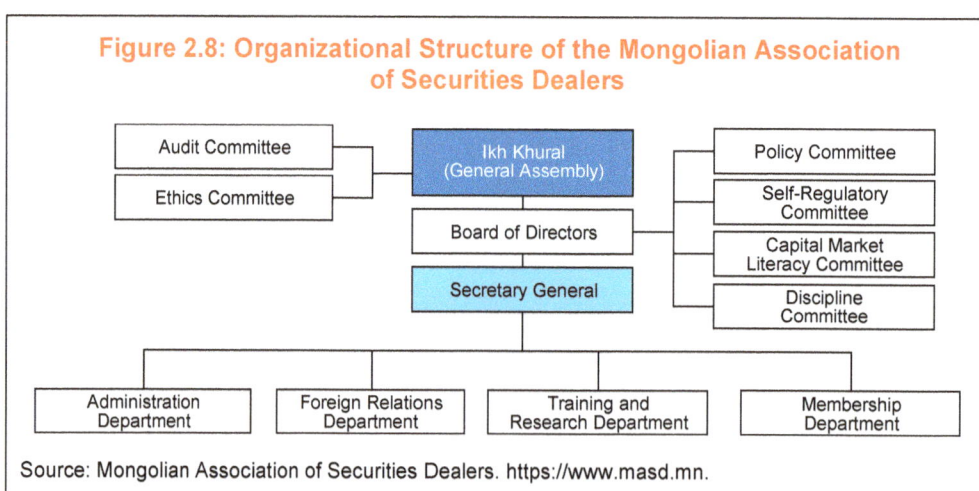

Figure 2.8: Organizational Structure of the Mongolian Association of Securities Dealers

Source: Mongolian Association of Securities Dealers. https://www.masd.mn.

E.   Regulatory Framework for Debt Securities

The regulatory framework for debt securities in the Mongolian capital market differs depending on whether the issuing body is the government or a private entity.

1.   Government Bonds

Government bonds are regulated under the Debt Management Law (enacted 18 February 2015). As per Article 26 of the Debt Management Law, the MOF is responsible for formulating regulations in the primary and secondary market for government securities. The Securities Market Law was amended on 18 February 2015 to remove government and municipal bonds from the list of securities regulated by the law.

The first regulation of government bonds, Regulation on Issuing and Settling Discounted Government Bonds, was approved on 26 September 1996 with Government Decree No. 246. Since then, multiple revisions have been made to government bond regulations in 1998, 2012, 2013, and 2014. The most notable of which was the 2014 Regulation on Issuance and Trading of Government Securities (Government Decree No. 371), which allowed for the issuance of government bonds to the public through an exchange in addition to off-exchange issuance through the BOM.

Exchange issuances of government bonds were regulated by the 2014 regulation and issued through the MSE, as per the MSE Guidance on Primary Market Issuance of Government Securities. The exchange issuance of government bonds was termed "retail government securities" in the 2014 regulation. The term was used for all government bond issuance until October 2017 when the MOF temporarily ceased LCY government bonds issuance.

On the other hand, off-exchange issuances of government bonds were organized through the BOM-operated interbank OTC market and were regulated by the Government Regulation and the Regulation on Issuance and Trading of Government Securities, approved as per the Joint Decree of the Minister of Finance and Governor of the Central Bank on 25 October 2012.

Secondary market trading of interbank OTC (off-exchange) government bonds was regulated by the 2013 Regulation on Secondary Market Trading of Government Securities, approved by the Joint Decree of the Minister of Finance, Governor of the Central Bank, and Chair of the Financial Regulatory Committee.

However, a new Regulation on Primary and Secondary Market Operations of Domestic Government Securities was approved by Government Decree No. 77 on 20 February 2019. The key change in the newly approved regulation lies in allowing the issuer (MOF) to choose the organizer of trading and removed the distinction between exchange issuance and off-exchange issuance.

In addition, primary market issuance and secondary market trading of government securities were now regulated by this single regulation instead of separate regulations previously. Pricing and issuance methods were regulated in more detail under this new regulation, including allowing for auction or negotiated issuance directly to the buyer. The term "retail government bond" was removed in the new regulation, meaning this country-specific term may not be used anymore when government bond issuance restarts in the future.

On 24 May 2017, the IMF approved a 3-year arrangement under the EFF for Mongolia, to support the country's economic reform program following a sharp decline in commodity prices and a slowdown in key export markets, according to the IMF.[9] The program included a broad set of structural reforms, as well as requirements for fiscal consolidation to restore debt sustainability. As a result, LCY government bond issuance was temporarily halted by the MOF in October 2017. Because the new 2019 government bond regulation was approved after this halt in LCY government bond issuance, it is yet to be implemented in practice.

With respect to retail investor government bonds becoming available to trade in 2015, the MSE organized the trading as per the MSE Listing Rules and the Guidance on Primary Market Issuance of Government Securities, approved as per Decree No. A/115 of the Chief Executive Officer (CEO) of the MSE.

2.   Corporate Debt Instruments

Public offerings of corporate debt instruments are regulated by the FRC, as per the Securities Market Law and the Company Law. The detailed regulatory process is outlined in Regulation on Securities Registration of the FRC (amended as per Resolution No. 408 on 23 November 2015).

In addition, public offerings of corporate debt securities (referred to as open or listed) are regulated by the Listing Rules and Trading Rules of the exchange. The listing of corporate debt securities is regulated under the MSE's Listing Rules (please see details in Chapter III). Primary and secondary trading takes place in accordance with the Trading Rules (approved 10 February 2012) and the new Primary Market Securities Issuance Rules (approved 26 October 2018) of the MSE.

For the MSX, corporate debt securities listings follow the MSX Listing Rules (please see details in Chapter III) and the MSX Trading Rules (approved 16 May 2018).

Privately placed corporate debt instruments (referred to as closed) are beyond the scope of the Securities Market Law and hence follow the Company Law. As the Securities Market Law regulates and defines securities in general, and privately placed corporate debt instruments are generally issued in practice with a purchasing agreement between the issuer, underwriter, and investors, these privately placed debt instruments are not be deemed securities under the current regulations.

However, if the privately placed corporate debt instruments are registered at a regulated securities depository entity (MCSD or a custodian), which are regulated by the FRC, then the debt instruments can be deemed as securities under the Securities Market Law. As per the law, registration at a depository entity counts as legal proof of ownership of the securities.

In addition, in accordance with the Securities Market Law, the private placement of securities issued by a company that has previously issued publicly offered securities is to be registered with the FRC. Hence, these privately placed securities are regulated by the Securities Market Law and the Regulation on Securities Registration of the FRC.

The Securities Market Law has no definition of the term "bond," while corporate bonds are termed "corporate debt instruments" under the law. As such, for the purpose of this bond market guide, publicly offered and FRC-regulated corporate debt instruments are termed corporate debt securities or instruments, while privately placed corporate debt instruments are termed debt instruments and not securities.

---

[9]   IMF. 2017. IMF Executive Board Approves Financial Arrangement for Mongolia. Press Release No. 17/193. 24 May. https://www.imf.org/en/News/Articles/2017/05/24/17193-imf-executive-board-approves-financial-arrangement-for-mongolia.

F.   Debt Securities Issuance Regulatory Processes

According to the Securities Market Law, public offers of securities are regulated by the FRC. The regulatory procedure for public offers of securities are outlined in the FRC Regulation on Securities Registration.

1.   Regulatory Process by Issuer Type

There is no distinction between corporate issuers and financial institution issuers in the Securities Market Law. However, certificates of deposit and short-term financial instruments issued on the money market with a maturity of less than 1 year by commercial banks are not regulated by this law.

Under the Securities Market Law, foreign issuers and domestic issuers are not separately distinguished, and there is no restriction on foreign issuers. There are, however, clauses regarding foreign-exchange-listed nonresident issuers trading its securities in Mongolia in the Securities Market Law. The specific requirements are to be decided by the FRC, according to the law.

To regulate and fast-track the process of allowing a foreign-exchange-listed nonresident issuer to issue its securities in Mongolia, the FRC has approved the Temporary Regulation on Registering Securities Offered in Mongolia by a Foreign Exchange Listed Entity and Securities Offered in a Foreign Country by a Mongolian Exchange Listed Entity on 24 November 2017. As a result, the first dual-listing at the MSE was completed in April 2018.

Government bonds are not regulated by the Securities Market Law and hence not regulated by the FRC. The government bond issuance process is regulated by the Debt Management Law and the MOF.

2.   Regulatory Process Overview

In the case of a public offer, the issuer is required to appoint an underwriter and prepare a securities prospectus to file with both the FRC and the exchange. Detailed requirements on the contents of the securities prospectus are outlined in the Securities Market Law as well as the FRC Regulation on Securities Registration.

In addition, the issuer is required to have an audited financial report, business and asset valuation report, and a legal opinion prepared by an audit firm, an asset valuation firm, and a legal firm. The underwriter, audit firm, asset valuation firm, and legal firm are all required to be licensed by the FRC since providing auditing services, valuation and appraisal services, and legal advice to participants in the securities market are all considered regulated activities under the Securities Market Law. A list of service providers with licenses can be found on the FRC website.[10]

Figure 2.9 provides an overview of the regulatory process for public offering of securities in the Mongolian capital market. Detailed explanations are provided in subsequent sections.

---

[10] http://www.frc.mn/?locale=en

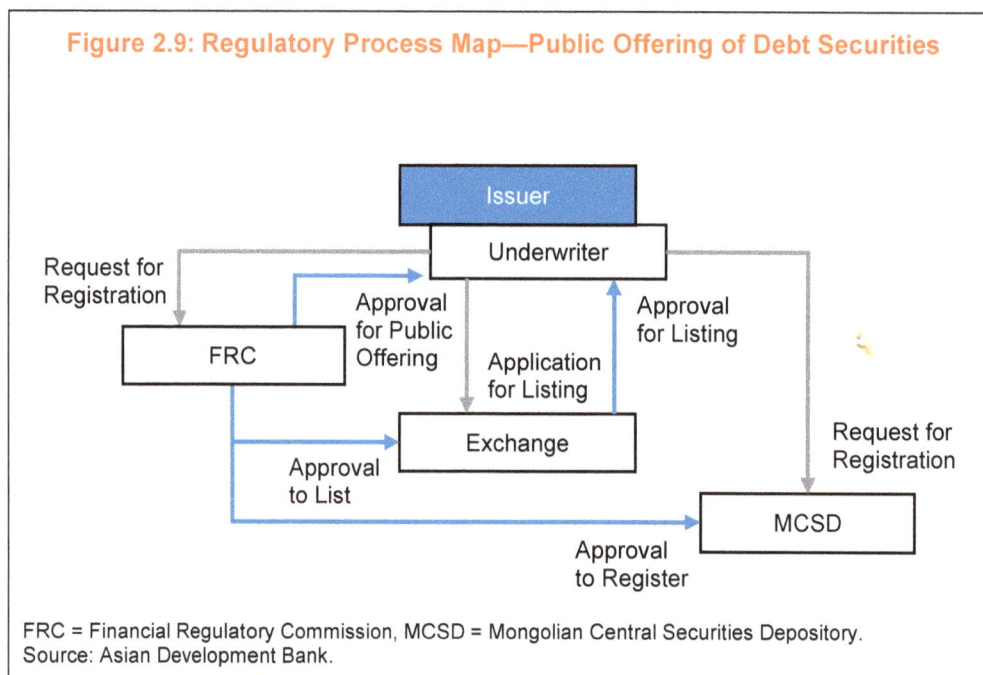

Figure 2.9: Regulatory Process Map—Public Offering of Debt Securities

FRC = Financial Regulatory Commission, MCSD = Mongolian Central Securities Depository.
Source: Asian Development Bank.

The issuer is required to get approval from both the FRC and the exchange to publicly offer its securities. Once the FRC approves the issuer to publicly offer its securities, the FRC adds it to the register of securities approved for public offer and sends approvals to list the securities on the exchange, as well as to the MCSD to register the securities. The exchange is required to approve the listing of the securities under the current regulations. The issuer is not required to receive a separate approval from the MCSD to register its securities approved by the FRC for public offer, although the issuer needs to send a formal request to the MCSD to register its securities.

Under the Securities Market Law and the FRC Regulation on Securities Registration, no distinction is made between equity and debt securities in general and hence all requirements for a public offering of equity is also applicable to debt securities. The most notable of which is the requirement to have business and asset valuation reports done by a licensed asset valuation firm regulated by the FRC. The business and asset valuation reports are specific to the Mongolian capital market and the requirement is expected to be removed in future amendment to the legislation.

3.   Regulatory Process for Public Offers

The process of offering corporate debt securities by public offer is regulated by the Securities Market Law, FRC Regulation on Securities Registration, and the Securities Listing Rules of the relevant exchange.

According to Article 16 of the Securities Market Law, the requirements to offer corporate debt instruments by public offer are as follows:

(i)   A company that has met the criteria determined by the FRC and the exchange may issue debt instruments for public offer.

(ii)   The total value of debt instruments for public offer being issued by a company shall not exceed the relevant company's net asset value. The total value of debt instruments for public offer being issued with a third-party guarantee shall not be greater than the total sum of the amount of the relevant company's net asset value and the total guarantees issued by the third party.

In addition, the following are required by the Securities Market Law from the issuer for securities issuance by public offer in general, not limited to debt instruments:

(i)   The securities issuer shall, either independently or based on a contract established with a regulated entity, offer its securities on the primary securities market by way of advertising and offering the securities to 50 or more investors.

(ii) When offering securities specified in Article 5.1.1 of this law to the public, the securities issuer shall engage a legal entity licensed to carry out underwriting activities.

(iii) When publicly offering securities, the securities issuer shall provide interested persons access to the relevant securities prospectus free of charge.

(iv) In the event that additional information are required from the securities issuer concerning registered securities that have been approved for public offer, or where it has been established that the securities issuer gave incomplete, false, or misleading information when registering the relevant securities and the securities were offered or misrepresentations were made on the basis of such information, then depending on the gravity of the violation, the FRC may adopt a resolution to either temporarily suspend the public offer or revoke the registration of the securities approved for public offer, notifying the securities issuer and the relevant stock exchange setting out justifiable grounds therefore and inform the public of the same.

(v)   The securities issuer shall be liable for costs and expenses and any loss or damage caused to others in connection with the revocation of the registration of securities approved for public offer resulting from the wrongful action of the securities issuer in accordance with Article 11.5 of this law.

(vi) It is prohibited to publicly offer shares that have not been registered in the register of securities and approved for public offer or to publicly offer shares of an LLC.

(vii) Securities that are registered both in the register of securities approved for public offer and in the stock exchange register shall be sold on the primary securities market.

(viii) The FRC shall issue permission to trade the securities on the primary securities market and such permission shall be granted on the basis of a request from the securities issuer and confirmation from the stock exchange that the securities are registered in the stock exchange register and the relevant preparations are finalized.

(ix) It is prohibited to use the funds raised by way of securities trading for purposes other than those specified in the relevant securities prospectus.

According to Article 10 of the Securities Market Law, a securities prospectus is not required for the following:

(i)   an issue of securities that are wholly guaranteed by the government;

(ii) a consolidation or split of issued shares;

(iii) a conversion of convertible debt instruments into shares in accordance with a securities prospectus previously circulated to the public; or

(iv) such other circumstances as may be provided in law.

The following is the step-by-step explanation of the regulatory process for the public offer of debt securities.

According to the Securities Market Law, for the public offer of securities, the issuer is required to appoint an underwriter licensed by the FRC. In addition, pursuant to Article 10 of the law, the securities prospectus is required to be prepared and needs to include an audited financial report, asset valuation report, and a legal opinion prepared by the relevant third-party advisors—an independent audit firm, asset valuation firm, and a legal firm, respectively.[11] The contents of the audit report, valuation report, and a legal opinion are outlined in the Securities Market Law, the FRC Regulation on Securities Registration, and the Listing Rules of the exchange.

The underwriter, audit firm, asset valuation firm, and legal firm are all required to be licensed by the FRC and independent from each other. Because these reports take time to prepare, the issuer needs to appoint the third-party advisors early in the public offer preparation stage. A list of service providers with licenses can be found on the FRC website.

To offer its securities by public offer, the issuer is required to appoint an underwriter licensed by the FRC to lead the entire securities issuance process. While the underwriter is expected to create and submit the prospectus and relevant application forms in practice, the responsibility for the submission of the required documents and the information contained lies with the issuer.

a.   Requirements Set by Law

The following documents shall be appended to an application to register securities in the register of securities approved for public offer, according to the Securities Market Law (amended 24 May 2013):

(i)   application form,
(ii)   securities prospectus,
(iii)   document evidencing payment of the regulatory service fee, and
(iv)   such other additional documents as specified in regulations issued by the FRC.

The securities prospectus is required to include the following information, according to Article 10.5 of the Securities Market Law:

(i)   name, permanent address, postal and contact address of the securities issuer, its industry and business activities, and whether it is registered with the stock exchange;
(ii)   state registration number and the registration date of the securities issuer;
(iii)   full name of any influential shareholder and, if a legal entity, the name, state registration number, and number and percentage of shares held by it and its connected persons;

---

[11] An asset valuation firm is an entity that provides property valuation and appraisal services under a special license. Typically, these firms provide asset valuation for the purposes of valuing collateral assets and asset appraisal for insurance purposes. For an asset valuation firm to provide valuation services to participants in the securities market, which is considered a regulated activity by law, it is required to be licensed by the FRC. In the context of the securities market, asset valuation firms provide a valuation report on properties and assets on the issuer's balance sheet as well as a business valuation report of the issuer as an enterprise. These requirements are specific to the Mongolian capital market and to the public offering of securities in general.

(iv)   information concerning the structure, organization, and governing persons of the securities issuer, and information concerning the number and percentage of shares held by such governing persons;

(v)   information concerning the amount of share capital of the securities issuer; the number, type, and par value of securities that were previously authorized, issued, and redeemed; the net asset value and information concerning the securities issuer's tangible and intangible assets;

(vi)   securities issuer's financial statements and an auditor's report in relation to the same;

(vii)   details of the contracts and transactions having a value of an amount equal to 5% or more of the share capital of the securities issuer, and information on performance and/or current status of the same;

(viii)   details of the connected persons of the securities issuer;

(ix)   number, type, and par value of securities being publicly offered, the conditions and procedures for any public offer and/or trade of these, the conditions and procedures for distributing dividends, and in the case of debt instruments, the details of the maturity term and the conditions and procedures for payment of the principal and interest;

(x)   rights and obligations attached to the securities being publicly offered;

(xi)   business plan specifying the use of the capital to be raised by issue of the securities;

(xii)   if a security is convertible into shares, the conditions and procedures for such conversion;

(xiii)   risks for the security issuer's operations and risk management plans;

(xiv)   list of regulated entities and other professional service providers involved in the public offer of the securities and the rights, obligations, and liabilities provided in the contracts entered into therewith;

(xv)   with respect to debt instruments, information regarding any guarantees for repayment and/or pledged property;

(xvi)   property valuation reports prepared within the past year; and

(xvii)   such other information considered by the FRC as necessary to include in the prospectus.

In addition, the securities prospectus is required to meet the following requirements, according to Article 10 of the Securities Market Law:

(i)   Securities must be subject to public offer within 6 months of the date of registration of the same and the related prospectus with the FRC. It is prohibited to publicly offer securities after the expiry of this period.

(ii)   The securities prospectus must include information regarding the securities issuer: its shareholders, management, organizational structure and governing persons, assets, debts, financial condition, present and future outlook, risks relating to the securities issuer, the securities being issued, the rights evidenced by such securities, the procedures for trading the securities, independent opinions, and such other information as the FRC may consider necessary for investors to make an investment decision.

(iii)   The securities prospectus shall be prepared in accordance with the procedures specified in Article 8.2 of this law.

(iv)   A law firm authorized to provide legal services in accordance with Article 33.2.1 of this law shall verify whether the information included in the securities prospectus is valid and accurate, and issue an opinion in relation thereto. A legal entity authorized to provide audit services in accordance with Article 33.2.3 of this law shall opine on the accuracy of the financial information.

(v)   The financial reports and legal opinion as verified by the entities specified in Article 33.2 of this law shall form an integral part of the securities prospectus.

(vi)   The application delivered to the FRC, the securities prospectus, and copies of the same shall be signed and verified by the chair of the board of directors, the executive director, and the chief financial officer of the securities issuer, the issuer of the legal opinion, the independent auditor that audited the financial report, and any other relevant independent experts.

(vii)   In the event there is a change in the information specified in Article 10.5 of this law, the securities issuer is under obligation to update the securities prospectus with the consent of the FRC, and it is prohibited for the securities issuer to amend the securities prospectus without the FRC's consent.

(viii) If, within the period specified in Article 10.1 of this law, there is any change to the circumstances of the securities issuer and/or the market conditions that could affect an investor's decision, the securities issuer shall inform the FRC concerning this and include an addendum to the securities prospectus relating to such change.

Furthermore, the application to register securities for public offer needs to meet the requirements set by the FRC and the exchange in accordance with the respective rules and regulations.

b.   Requirements Set by FRC Regulations

According to the FRC Regulation on Securities Registration (amended 23 November 2015, effective 1 January 2016), the following documents are required to be appended to an application to register securities for public offer:

(i)   application form for securities registration (Form FRC03101);

(ii)   securities prospectus prepared in accordance with the requirements set by the exchange;

(iii)   shareholders' decision to issue securities, or make changes to its securities, along with related evidence;

(iv)   legal opinion required by the Section 4.2.2 of the FRC regulation;

(v)   business and asset valuation report, and audit report prepared in accordance with the requirements set by the exchange;

(vi)   the report of a third-party analyst or professional, if a third-party analyst or professional has conducted a research report in accordance with Section 10.8 of the Securities Market Law; and

(vii)   a document evidencing payment of the regulatory service fee.

In addition, according to Section 4.2.2 of the FRC Regulation on Securities Registration, the legal opinion prepared by the FRC-licensed legal firm needs to reflect the following issues:

(i)   whether the issuer is created and registered in accordance with the law;

(ii)   the management skills and experience of the board, executive management, and authorized officers of the issuer, whether they meet the requirements set by the Mongolian Corporate Governance Code approved by the FRC, and whether they have been involved in criminal activities;

(iii)   whether the issuer's rules and internal regulations are in compliance with applicable law and the Mongolian Corporate Governance Code approved by the FRC;

(iv)   whether the sale and purchase, supply, loan and other agreements, and contracts of significant importance to the issuer are in compliance with applicable law;

(v)   whether significant and conflict-of-interest transactions made in the last 3 years have been made in accordance with applicable laws and regulations;

(vi)   whether there are any circumstances that could substantially affect the issuer's activities, including licensing of operations, licenses, copyrights, patents, trademarks and services, their expiration, termination, or obligation to ensure fulfillment of any obligations;

(vii)   whether the ownership of securities, immovable property, or other property is valid, or whether it has an obligation to fulfill any obligations;

(viii) whether the information specified in the securities registration application and securities prospectus is evidenced with valid documents; and

(ix)   identify the person who exercises control of the issuer based on information on the company's parent, daughter, sister, or related companies.

Moreover, the FRC requires the issuer to submit all contracts and agreements between the issuer and the third-party advisors (underwriter, audit firm, legal firm, and valuation firm) to review whether the contracts have been signed in accordance with the relevant laws and whether the roles and responsibilities of each party have been properly defined.

c.   Requirements Set by the MSE Listing Rules

According to the MSE Listing Rules (approved 25 January 2018), the following documents are required to be appended to an application to list securities for public offer, as per Article 3.2:

(i)   application form for securities listing (Form 2);

(ii)   issuer's declaration (Form 3);

(iii)   underwriter's declaration (Form 4);

(iv)   listing decision by the issuer's competent authority;

(v)   securities prospectus;

(vi)   legal opinion as specified in Article 2.6 of the MSE Listing Rules;

(vii)   valuation report as specified in Article 2.7 of the MSE Listing Rules;

(viii) conclusions and opinions as specified in Article 2.4 of the MSE Listing Rules, where applicable; and

(ix)   a document evidencing payment of the listing application fee as specified in Article 22.2.1 of the MSE Listing Rules.

For the legal opinion required by Article 3.2 of the MSE Securities Listing Rules, the legal firm shall provide an opinion with regard to the following issues, as per Article 2.6 of the MSE Listing Rules:

(i)   whether there exists any violation in relation to the company state registration, tax, and social insurance payer account;

(ii)   whether the company charter and the draft company charter for a company undertaking an initial public offering and other internal rules and regulations comply with the relevant legislation and the "Corporate Governance Codex" issued by the FRC;

(iii)   whether the agreements in relation to procurement, sales, and loan and other agreements and contracts that are significant to the issuer's operations comply with relevant legislation; whether there exists any situation that may have potential adverse impacts on company operations;

(iv)   whether the large-scale transactions and transactions with conflicts of interest concluded during the preceding year are compliant with the relevant regulations;

(v)   whether the operational special permits, licenses, copyrights, patents, trademarks, and land use or ownership rights are valid, and whether there is any condition that may have potential adverse impacts on company operations relating to the abovementioned rights such as near-term expiration, cancellation, or pledge to the performance of obligation;

(vi)   whether the ownership rights pertaining to its securities holdings and its movable and immovable properties are valid, and whether there is any pledge by these to the performance of an obligation; and

(vii)   if the issuer belongs to the group structure as specified in Article 6.13 of the Company Law, the person exercising control of the issuer needs to be determined based on the information of the parent company, subsidiaries, affiliates, and dependent companies.

For the valuation report required by Article 3.2 of the MSE Securities Listing Rules, the following requirement is set out as per Article 2.8:

> The issuer shall sign a contract with an asset valuation firm as specified in Provision 33.2.2 of the Securities Markets Law and have the asset and business valuation performed and, in the case of the issuance of debt securities, have the asset valuation performed for the assets guaranteeing the repayment of the debt.

In addition, the audit firm is required to provide an opinion with regard to the following issues, as per Article 2.8 of the Listing Rules:

(i)   accounts for the most recent financial year shall be audited and an audit report provided;

(ii)   whether the company's accounting policies and financial reports comply with the International Financial Reporting Standards (IFRS); and

(iii)   whether the financial statement information contained in the securities prospectus is true and valid.

According to Article 4.2 of the MSE Securities Listing Rules, the securities prospectus shall consist of three parts: (i) "Issuer's Information," (ii) "Information on the Securities to Be Issued," and (iii) "Information on Parties Involved in Securities Issuance."

The Issuer's Information part of the securities prospectus shall contain the following information, as per Article 4.3 of the MSE Securities Listing Rules:

(i)   issuer's name, address, contact address, operational type, whether the issuer is listed on other exchanges, and, in cases of foreign-listed issuers, the information about the home exchange;

(ii)   issuer's state registration, register number, and the date of registration;

(iii)   issuer's influential shareholders' names, surnames, and positions held; in case of a legal person, its name, state registration number, and if it belongs to a group structure; information about the companies belonging to the group, control structure, and the number and percentage of shareholdings held individually or with related persons; and information about the related persons;

(iv)   issuer's organizational structure, information about its competent persons, and the number and percentage of their shareholdings in the company;

(v)   issuer's share capital; number, type, and nominal price of the declared, issued, and repurchased securities; amount of equity and tangible and intangible assets;

(vi)   issuer's financial report and audit report;

(vii)   agreements and contracts where the issuer is responsible for payment of more than 5% of its share capital and information about their performance;

(viii) issuer's related persons;

(ix)   market share of the issuer in the market of its primary operation and information about its competitors;
(x)   dividend policy approved by the company's competent authority;
(xi)   business plan for the use of the proceeds from the securities issuance;
(xii)   overview of medium-term business plan; and
(xiii) risks to the issuer's operations and risk management plan.

The Information on the Securities to Be Issued part of the securities prospectus shall contain the following information, as per Article 4.4 of the MSE Securities Listing Rules:

(i)   type, quantity, class, and nominal price of the securities to be offered to the public; the conditions for offering and trading, in case of debt securities, the duration, principal amount, and coupon payment policy and payment rules;
(ii)   rights and responsibilities attached to the securities being offered to the public;
(iii)   conditions and rules for conversion in case of convertible securities; and
(iv)   repayment guarantee and collateral information in case of debt securities.

The Information on Parties Involved in Securities Issuance part of the securities prospectus shall contain information on the following, as per Article 4.5 of the MSE Securities Listing Rules:

(i)   regulated person and other persons providing professional services involved in the securities offering; and
(ii)   rights, responsibilities, and liabilities in accordance with the contracts signed with these persons.

In addition, the following documents shall be attached to the securities prospectus, as per Article 4.8 of the MSE Securities Listing Rules:

(i)   notarized copy of state registration certificate;
(ii)   copy of the company charter registered in the state registrar and the decision to make amendments to the charter following the offering of securities and the draft charter;
(iii)   copy of the decision to issue securities by a competent authority;
(iv)   copy of an agreement signed with a market maker where applicable;
(v)   information on parent company, subsidiaries, and dependent companies and copies of relevant documents to prove the relations;
(vi)   profile of company's authorized persons and proof of their experience sufficient to run company operations;
(vii)   information on the person in charge of securities and exchange communications and their contact details;
(viii) copies of the contracts signed with the parties specified in Articles 2.1, 2.2, and 2.4 of the MSE Listing Rules and the reports and opinions specified in Articles 2.6, 2.7, and 2.8;
(ix)   proof of compliance of the company's board of directors with the requirements set out in Articles 75, 79, and 81 of the Company Law;
(x)   proof of adoption of the corporate governance principles (codex) that is accepted domestically and internationally; in case of the absence of an adoption of the codex, proof of the approval of the internal governance regulations for the purposes of compliance with the codex, and proof of the company's authorized persons' compliance with the requirements set out in Article 75.8 of the Company Law; and
(xi)   other documents and evidence to prove the information contained in the prospectus.

The MSE Listing Rules have the following requirements regarding the securities prospectus, as per Article 4:

(i)   On the first page of the prospectus shall be the following warning in bold letters: "Be advised that the Mongolian Stock Exchange's approval of the listing of the securities does not constitute any guarantee on the risks of the securities. Be warned that the purchase of these securities is ALWAYS RISKY for you as an investor and be reminded to make your investment decision after careful examination of the securities prospectus and securities issuance procedure."

(ii)   The securities prospectus shall be signed and sealed by the issuer's chair of the board of directors, CEO, chief accountant, and the underwriter's CEO and shall contain a declaration stating: "The securities prospectus submitted to the Stock Exchange is the same as the one submitted to the Financial Regulatory Commission and does not contain any inconsistency."

(iii)   The securities prospectus shall be no more than 400 pages and shall be a document filed and bound, including table of contents.

(iv)   All the pages of the securities prospectus shall be paged and each page shall be signed and dated by the issuer's CEO and the underwriter's CEO on the bottom right corner.

(v)   If the securities prospectus is produced in a foreign language, a Mongolian translation by an accredited body shall be attached.

(vi)   The issuer shall submit to the exchange two printed originals of the listing application, securities prospectus and other documents that comply with the requirements set out in the MSE Listing Rules.

With regard to rules concerning corporate debt instruments, the MSE Listing Rules have the following requirements, as per Articles 8 and 14:

(i)   Debt securities shall be listed by the name of the instrument and the name shall contain the maturity, coupon rate, and coupon payment frequency.

(ii)   There shall be no restrictions on the free movement and trading of the securities, such as a pledge, and the seal shall be freely transferable and tradable.

(iii)   The value of the debt securities offered to the public shall meet the conditions set out in Article 16.4 of the Securities Markets Law.

(iv)   In the case of convertible securities, the shares for future conversion shall be listed on the exchange and shall meet the requirements and conditions set out in Article 39 of the Company Law.

(v)   In the case of offering debt securities, an underwriter may not be required depending on the scale of offering and the nature of the issuer.

(vi)   The issuer may be required to provide collateral for the property and property rights or provide a guarantee by an independent third party in case the exchange considers the debt securities to have potential adverse impacts on the rights and interests of the investor.

In addition, the issuer of corporate debt securities shall meet the criteria for a Board II listing, which states the following as per Article 12 of the MSE Listing Rules:

(i)   The issuer shall have stable operations in its industry for a minimum of 2 years prior to the date of listing application.

(ii)   The financial reports for the most recent 2 financial years shall be prepared in accordance with the IFRS and verified by an auditing firm along with an audit report. In the case of a foreign-listed issuer listed on an exchange approved by the FRC, the financial reports are accepted if prepared in accordance with a different accounting standard that is accepted by the foreign (nonresident) exchange. In such cases, the issuer shall report material changes on the financial report that are caused by the difference between the IFRS and the accounting standard in which the reports are originally prepared.

(iii)   The issuer shall have sufficient working capital and current assets minus short-term liabilities for running its business operations for at least 12 months after the listing or must have a net profit of no less than MNT100 million.

(iv)   The issuer shall comply with the corporate governance principles or explain if it is not in compliance.

However, if the issuer fails to meet the criteria specified in Article 12 of the MSE Listing Rules, then the issuer is required to meet any of the following criteria, as per Article 14.2:

(i)   the issuer shall have conducted its main operations for no less than 3 years and hold sufficient collateral assets to guarantee full repayment of the principal and interest payments for the debt securities; or

(ii)   the issuer shall be fully guaranteed by the Government of Mongolia; or

(iii) the debt securities offered to the public shall be insured by more than 80% of its total value.

In addition, certain waivers from the listing requirements can be made by the order of the CEO of the MSE, if a request to waive has been made by the issuer or the underwriter with the supporting arguments in accordance with Article 15 of the MSE Securities Listing Rules.

According to Article 9.3 of the MSE Listing Rules, these rules are not applicable to the debt securities issued by foreign-listed issuers, debt securities denominated in a foreign currency, and debt securities previously issued on a foreign (nonresident) exchange.

d.   Requirements Set by the MSX Listing Rules

According to the MSX Listing Rules (approved 24 May 2018), the following requirements must be met for the issuance of debt instruments, as per Article 16:

(i)   The issuer (and in the case of issuance of secured debt instruments, the issuer and the guarantor) shall be properly established and registered in accordance with the procedures established by the relevant legislation of the country of origin.

(ii)   If the issuer (and in the case of issuance of secured debt instruments, the issuer and the guarantor) are not listed on the exchange, their business is required to be considered suitable by the exchange.

(iii) The issuer has been operating for at least 3 years.

(iv)   The issuer (and in the case of issuance of secured debt instruments, the issuer and the guarantor) shall submit to the exchange audited financial statements for the last 3 years. In special cases, the exchange may accept 2-year financial statements.

(v)   New applicants must submit registration documents to the exchange within 6 months of the submission of the previous year's financial statements.

(vi)   The issuer (and in the case of issuance of secured debt instruments, the equity capital of the guarantor) shall be not less than MNT1 billion and the nominal value of the debt instrument shall not be less than MNT500 million. This requirement does not apply if additional debt instruments are being issued.

(vii) A person purchasing a debt instrument shall have the right to freely dispose of its debt instruments.

(viii) The issuer may issue debt instruments with conditions of conversion into shares.

(ix) If the issuer issues a convertible debt instrument, it must fully comply with the requirements set forth in Article 39 of the Company Law.

The following documents are required to be submitted to the MSX for the review of application for listing:

(i) two copies of the draft registration document with the complete inclusion of the relevant information specified in Chapter XVIII and Appendix 6-A of the MSX Listing Rules;

(ii) two copies of the draft official notice;

(iii) two copies of the draft debt instrument purchase order sheet;

(iv) two copies of documents and guarantees prepared in accordance with Appendix 4 of the MSX Listing Rules;

(v) two copies of the statement of adjustment by a certified accountant if an adjustment has been made to the certified accountant's opinion;

(vi) a certified copy of financial statements, correction statements, the real estate valuation report, the contract, and the official decision;

(vii) a proof of commitment signed by each member of the issuer's board and each authorized person regarding their biography;

(viii) the debt instrument guarantee and other related documents;

(ix) a certified copy of the state registration certificate or its equivalent;

(x) a certified copy of an operating permit;

(xi) a certified copy of the company's charter, memorandum, and similar documents; and

(xii) an application form made in accordance with the Form 3-3.

The detailed requirements for the application form and related documents are set out in Section 7 of the MSX Listing Rules.

Step 3—Review of Registration Application by FRC and the Exchange

The FRC shall review and issue a decision within 20 working days of receipt of the required documents and the securities prospectus, according to Article 9.6 of the Securities Market Law. When a decision refusing to register the securities has been made by the FRC, it must specify justifiable grounds for the decision. The period for considering applications shall be calculated as commencing on the date of receipt of a complete application.

However, the period for considering applications may be extended by up to a maximum of 15 working days by the FRC if deemed necessary to obtain additional documents, valuations, or other reports from the issuer or independent experts and advisors as per the law.

The exchange shall review and issue a decision whether to accept or refuse the securities listing application within 14 working days, according to Article 3.2.3 of the FRC Regulation on Securities Registration. If a decision to accept the listing has been made, it must deliver the decision along with its opinion to the FRC within 2 working days.

Based on the FRC's decision to register the securities, the actual securities registration is made at the FRC, the exchange, and the central depository. A securities trading code is issued by the exchange, while an International Securities Identification Number is issued by the MCSD.

Step 4—Announcement and Offering Period

When the security is approved by the FRC for public offer, the decision is delivered to the issuer, the exchange, and the MCSD, and the decision is made public through the FRC website.

The issuer and underwriter are then required to submit a primary market offering plan to the exchange to be approved, and a request to start the primary market offering is made to the FRC. The request to the FRC is needed to be made more than 3 working days prior to the actual start of the public offering. A detailed offering schedule is required to be outlined in the request and the offering period shall not be longer than 1 month since the commencement of the public offer, as per the FRC Regulation on Securities Registration.

After the commencement of the public offering is approved by the FRC, the issuer and the underwriter are allowed to start a public offer of the securities for sale. The issuer and the underwriter are required to provide investors with free access to required information at no cost, as per the Securities Market Law. Only the information contained in the securities prospectus approved by the FRC is allowed to be marketed to the public.

Since the date of the securities registration by the FRC, the issuer and its underwriter have 6 months to offer the securities to the public and start primary market issuance of the securities. If the 6-month period is expired, the registration of the securities for public offer is terminated as per the Securities Market Law.

Step 5—Closing Offer and Primary Market Issuance

The offering closes at the date and time set in the Primary Market Offering Plan approved by the exchange, and as per the schedule outlined in the primary issuance request sent to and approved by the FRC.

The primary market issuance of the securities is conducted by the method outlined in the securities prospectus approved by the FRC and the exchange. The underwriter conducts book-building operations in the method approved by the exchange.

After the primary market issuance is completed, the underwriter is required to submit a trading report to the FRC within 3 working days, as outlined in the FRC Regulation on Securities Registration. The secondary market trading cannot commence until the FRC approves the primary market issuance as successful, and generally, there are a few days of gap between them.

If the FRC decides that the primary market issuance does not meet the requirements set in the FRC Regulation on Securities Registration and the relevant laws, it can invalidate and cancel the primary market issuance. The FRC deems the primary market offer successful if all funds necessary to be raised by the public offer have been transferred to the respective account of the issuer, as per the Securities Market Law. Once the offer is deemed successful by the FRC, the secondary market trading can commence.

Step 6—Securities Distribution and Commencement of Secondary Market Trading

If the FRC decides that the primary market offer was successful, it is then required to deliver its approval to conduct securities ownership registration to the MCSD and approval to start secondary market trading to the exchange, in writing, within 3 working days, according to the FRC Regulation on Securities Registration. The exchange then decides and announces the date of secondary market trading commencement. Once the secondary market trading has started, investors can freely trade the securities on the open market.

Due to these steps required by the FRC Regulation on Securities Registration, there is typically a gap of a few days between primary market issuance and secondary market trading of the publicly offered securities.

4. Regulatory Process for Private Placements

The Security Market Law has no provision on private placements, except for when private placement of securities issued by a company that has previously issued publicly offered securities, which are required to be registered with the FRC. In this case, these privately placed securities would need to follow the security registration process outlined in the FRC Regulation on Securities Registration. Otherwise, any private placement of securities in the private market (referred as closed) by limited liability companies would follow the Company Law, and FRC regulations would not apply.

Issuance of corporate debt instruments by private placement in the Mongolian capital market is done in practice by multiparty agreements between the issuer, the underwriter, and the investor or buyer. The issuer can choose to use a custodian or central depository for the settlement and registration of the debt instruments, but generally the corporate debt instruments are not registered, and settlements are done by the underwriter.

In the case of government bonds, private placements and direct issuance are regulated by the Debt Management Law and the 2019 Regulation on Primary and Secondary Market Operations of Domestic Government Securities.

5. Regulatory Process in Case of a Nonresident Issuer

The Securities Market Law does not make a distinction between nonresident and domestic issuers and there are no restrictions on nonresident issuers. There are, however, clauses in the Securities Market Law regarding a foreign-exchange-listed nonresident issuer issuing its securities. The specific requirements are decided by the FRC, in accordance with the law.

The FRC approved the Temporary Regulation on Registering Securities Offered in Mongolia by a Foreign Exchange Listed Entity and Securities Offered in a Foreign Country by Mongolian Exchange Listed Entity, on 24 November 2017. This allows fast-tracking of a public offer by foreign issuers listed on the FRC approved list of foreign (nonresident) exchanges that are regulated by the International Organization of Securities Commissions member regulator. The regulatory process is simpler because the listing request is not required to have business and asset valuation reports and an underwriter's opinion. It is still required to have a legal opinion by a licensed entity and an audited financial report. The documents are required to be translated into Mongolian, but only the original language version has legal authority and is required to be submitted as well.

Under this regulation, a foreign-exchange-listed nonresident issuer can submit its request for securities listing to the FRC and the MSE at the same time, and is only allowed to offer its securities on the public market after it has been approved by the FRC and after it has been registered at the FRC and the MCSD.

The FRC is required to reach a conclusion on whether to approve and register the security or not in under 20 working days, as per the regulation. However, this deadline can be extended another 15 working days if the FRC deems it requires additional information to reach a decision.

However, this regulation has been developed with an equity listing in mind, and it is unclear whether it can be applied to a public offering of debt securities.

6. Obligations After Approval and After Issuance

Issuers of publicly offered corporate debt securities are subject to several reporting requirements following the issuance of the securities.

An issuer is prohibited to use the funds raised by way of public offering of securities for purposes other than those specified in the securities prospectus, according to Article 12.9 of the Securities Market Law.

According to Article 20 of the Securities Market Law, a securities issuer must

(i) discuss and adopt a resolution to issue securities by a meeting of those suitably authorized;

(ii) produce information and reports connected with the trade in securities accurately and in accordance with relevant methodology in the approved form, and submit these to the FRC and issue these to the public within the prescribed period;

(iii) have no fewer independent members of the board of directors than as is specified in the Company Law of Mongolia;

(iv) appoint or elect suitable persons as governing persons;

(v) inform the public and shareholders in a timely fashion in the event that the implementation of a project provided in the securities prospectus has changed;

(vi) submit to the FRC and the stock exchange semiannual financial reports and annual financial reports certified by auditors registered with the FRC within the period specified in Article 13 of the Law on Accounting;

(vii) publish information concerning the operational and financial condition of the company in accordance with the procedures established by the FRC;

(viii) immediately inform the public of the resolutions of a shareholders' meeting and submit to the FRC and the stock exchange the relevant documents and information within 3 business days of such meetings;

(ix) immediately inform the public in the event of circumstances that could appreciably influence the price or trading volume of securities; and

(x) observe the corporate governance principles issued by the FRC.

Note that the corporate debt securities are not treated differently by the Securities Market Law in general, and these requirements are applicable to all securities issuers in the public market.

In the case of obligations set by the FRC Regulation on Securities Registration, Article 3.1 requires that the issuer

(i) comply with the corporate governance code;

(ii) shall be obliged to register the pledge of the debt instrument with the state registration authority of the pledged property; and

(iii) shall be obliged to keep all relevant documents related to securities registration, such as the securities prospectus, its supporting documents and independent expert opinions submitted to the FRC and the exchange for 10 years from the date of the FRC decision to register the securities.

According to Article 21 of the MSE Listing Rules, the securities issuer has the following ongoing obligation while it is listed on the exchange:

(i)   The issuer shall continue to meet the criteria specified in these rules for listing shares and debt securities during the time that its securities are listed on the exchange.

(ii)   The financial reports shall be prepared accurately in accordance with the IFRS and shall be regularly verified by an approved auditing company.

(iii)   The issuer shall comply with the relevant legislation, rules, regulations, and decisions for corporate actions such as the organization of shareholders' meetings and allocation of dividends. Such corporate actions shall be organized in Mongolian territory either by the issuer or by its authorized representative.

(iv)   The issuer shall have a dedicated securities specialist in charge of disseminating information pertaining to the securities to the public, and ensure implementation of the duties to shareholders and authorized bodies.

(v)   The issuer shall comply with the corporate governance principles or explain to the shareholders and the public in case of noncompliance with the principles. The issuer listed on Board I shall be fully compliant with corporate governance principles.

(vi)   The issuer shall implement the duties specified in the listing agreement signed with the exchange throughout the time that the issuer is listed on the exchange.

(vii)   The issuer shall inform the public and the exchange of its operations, financial situation, and any information that may have an impact on the price and trading activity of the securities as per the law and the relevant regulations from the FRC. In the case of a foreign-listed issuer, it shall follow Article 7.1 for publishing information.

7.   Regulatory Process for Domestic Financial Institution

The Securities Market Law does not differentiate financial institutions from other corporate issuers and therefore all regulations concerning public offer of securities are similarly applicable to domestic financial institutions.

However, financial instruments (securities) with a maturity of less than 1 year (commercial paper) issued by a commercial bank to be traded on a money market in accordance with Article 15.2 of the Banking Law are not regulated by the Securities Market Law, as per Article 5.2.

According to Article 15 of the Banking Law, commercial banks may issue, purchase, or pledge securities with a maturity of less than 1 year and that are traded in the money market with the approval of the BOM. For commercial banks to receive approval from the Central Bank, the bank is required to have met certain requirements, and receive a special license from the BOM. Specifically, the bank is required to have consistently met the prudential ratios of bank operations for the past 6 months, obtained a "good" or higher rating on the most recent inspection conducted by the BOM, and fulfilled the tasks assigned according to the inspection in a timely manner. Once the bank obtains the license, it can register the securities at the MCSD and trade its securities on the money market.

8.   Regulatory Process for Foreign-Currency-Denominated Debt Instruments

There are no specific regulations for foreign-currency-denominated debt instruments in Mongolia. The law does not forbid the issuance of securities in foreign currency.

However, according to Article 4 of the Law On Conducting Settlements In National Currency (enacted 9 July 2009), the price of goods, work, and services shall be expressed and settlement shall be conducted only in the national currency within the territory of Mongolia, and it is prohibited to set a price, carry out settlements, and run an advertisement in foreign currencies or settlement units without official BOM approval, except for bank and non-banking financial institution (NBFI) loans, deposits, and related services.

Previously, there have been instances of foreign-currency-denominated privately placed corporate debt instruments in the domestic market. Although these corporate debt instruments were denominated in a foreign currency, the underwriting service and related fees were settled in the national currency.

G.   Continuous Disclosure Requirements in the Mongolian Bond Market

1.   Summary of Continuous Disclosure for Mongolian Companies

Companies in Mongolia are required to submit financial statements to the MOF in accordance with the Law on Accounting (amended 19 June 2015). These statements are not made public.

Only companies with their securities trading in the public market are required to meet certain disclosure requirements set forth in the relevant laws and regulations. Private placements are not regulated in Mongolia; therefore, there are no disclosure requirements for private placements of corporate debt instruments.

According to Article 10 of the Law on Accounting, each year companies are required to submit half-year financial statements by 20 July and annual financial statements by 10 February to the MOF in digital form. The regulations and rules set by the FRC and exchanges follow the Law on Accounting for financial statement disclosure requirements.

2.   Disclosure for Public Offers and Listing of Corporate Debt Securities

a.   Requirements Set by Law

According to Article 20 of the Securities Market Law, a securities issuer has the following general obligations:

(i)   produce information and reports connected with the trade in securities accurately and in accordance with relevant methodology in the approved form, and submit these to the FRC and issue these to the public within the prescribed period;

(ii)   inform the public and shareholders in a timely fashion in the event that the implementation of a project provided in the securities prospectus has changed;

(iii)   submit to the FRC and the stock exchange semiannual financial reports and annual financial reports certified by auditors registered with the FRC within the period specified in the Law on Accounting;

(iv)   publish information concerning the operational and financial condition of the company in accordance with the procedures established by the FRC;

(v)   immediately inform the public of the resolutions of a shareholders' meeting and submit to the FRC and the stock exchange the relevant documents and information within 3 business days of such meetings; and

(vi)   immediately inform the public in the event of circumstances that could appreciably influence the price or trading volume of securities.

In addition, according to Article 56 of the Securities Market Law, the following information disclosure requirements are enforced on the securities issuer of securities being traded on the secondary market, to be notified to the FRC, the exchange, and through its website to the public within 1 business day of the circumstances arising:

(i)   where there are changes to the management structure of the securities issuer;

(ii)   where there is a change in the shareholding structure of the influential shareholder of a securities issuer, or where there are changes in the shareholding interests held by such influential shareholders in other companies;

(iii)   where there is any organizational change in the securities issuer, its subsidiaries, affiliates, and sister companies;

(iv)   where assets of the security issuer have been seized or confiscated;

(v)   where the securities issuer commences engaging in licensed activities, or where its license is suspended or revoked;

(vi)   where the shareholders' meetings of the securities issuer adopt resolutions; and

(vii)   any other circumstance that may influence the market price of the securities.

Corporate debt securities are not treated differently by the Securities Market Law in general, and these requirements are applicable to all securities issuers in the public market.

b.   Requirements Set by Financial Regulatory Commission Regulations

According to the FRC Regulation on Information Transparency of Security Issuers (approved 17 December 2015), issuers of securities in the public market are required to publicly disclose periodic reports in the form of semiannual and annual reports, and are required to publish them before 1 August and 1 April, respectively.

Article 2.3 of the Regulation on Information Transparency of Security Issuers outlines the information required to be included in the annual report as the following:

(i)   information on business operations of the company, including implementation results of the company strategies, industry standing, significant events during the reporting period, and social responsibilities;

(ii)   information on company management, including changes made in the management composition and structure; information on the company board, executive management, and their shareholding; and the implementation of a corporate governance code approved by the FRC;

(iii)   information on company financial statements, including analysis made on financial statements, audited statements, debts and their repayments, and information on significant and conflict-of-interest transactions;

(iv)   information on shareholders, including beneficiary owner, changes in influential shareholders, and decisions of shareholder meetings;

(v)   information on dividends, including dividend policy, results of dividend distribution, and if no dividend is paid their reasons and explanations; and

(vi)   other relevant information, including information deemed necessary by the company.

Article 3.2 outlines the information required to be disclosed in a timely manner, within 1 working day of the event occurring, as the following:

(i)   financial information, such as transactions that have a significant effect on company operations, assets, or financial standing; information on significant or conflict-of-interest transactions; sale and purchase of assets totaling more than 10% of the company assets; and if the company or its related parties become insolvent;

(ii) nonfinancial information, such as changes or delays in company operations, transfer of operations to related entities, changes in patents and copyrights, changes in name and address, changes in more than 15% of the workforce, changes in management, litigation information, changes in company registration, and changes in shareholding; and

(iii) information on management, such as a shareholder meeting announcement and its decisions, decisions made by the board that may affect securities prices, changes in composition of the board, and changes in an influential shareholder.

The company is required to disclose this information through its own website and the official website of the exchange and is held responsible for the accuracy of the information. The exchange is required to enforce and monitor the implementation of this regulation, as per Article 1.6 of the regulation.

Note that the corporate debt securities are not treated differently by the Securities Market Law and the relevant regulations in general, and these requirements are applicable to all securities issuers in the public market.

c.   Requirements Set by Exchange Rules

According to Article 21 of the MSE Listing Rules, the issuer is required to have a dedicated securities specialist in charge of disseminating information pertaining to the securities to the public and to inform the public and the exchange about its operations, financial situation, and any information that may have an impact on the price and trading activity of the securities as per the law and the relevant regulations from the FRC.

Detailed requirements and guidelines on the content of disclosure information, their timeline, and methods are outlined in the MSE Guidelines on Submitting Information Electronically for Listed Companies (approved 28 April 2017).

Company financial statements and semiannual and annual report contents and schedules follow the relevant laws and FRC regulations. All other information are required to be submitted in a timely manner, within 1 working day of the occurrence of the event. The company can submit the information in English on a voluntary basis.

According to Article 7.1 of the MSE Listing Rules, a foreign-listed issuer may follow the laws, rules, and regulations of the country and exchange of primary listing when submitting any reports or information to the FRC and the MSE. All the information and documents provided to the foreign (nonresident) exchange and regulator shall be submitted simultaneously to the MSE with a Mongolian translation on a regular basis (where necessary, the brief summary of the information in Mongolian can be provided). In case of a time difference due to the geographic location of the MSE and the foreign (nonresident) exchange, the information may be released on the foreign (nonresident) exchange first with the simultaneous submission of the information through e-mail to the MSE. The MSE shall publish the information to the public at the start of the following business day.

According to Article 1.19 of the MSX Listing Rules, the issuer is required to submit, in a timely manner, all types of information that the exchange deems necessary to protect investor interests and ensure normal market operation.

3.   Disclosure Requirements for Private Placement of Corporate Debt Instruments

Private placements of corporate debt instruments are not regulated by the Securities Market Law. Therefore, there are no specific disclosure requirements for private placements of corporate debt instruments. However, in the case of private placement of securities by a company that has previously issued publicly offered securities, the Securities Market Law requires that these securities be registered with the FRC. In this case, the issuer would be required to follow the disclosure requirements set forth by the relevant FRC regulations for public companies.

H.   Self-Regulatory Organizations and Market Participant Organizations

According to Article 69 of the Securities Market Law, a self-regulatory organization (SRO) is a legal entity registered with the FRC—and specified as a stock exchange, securities clearing house, securities central depository institution, or a professional association—that has a membership consisting of regulated legal entities and certified professionals specified in the Securities Market Law. The members of an SRO shall be a licensed and regulated entity that is registered with the FRC.

1.   Self-Regulatory Organizations

a.   Mongolian Stock Exchange

Established in 1991 for the purposes of privatizing state-owned enterprises and promoting the development of the capital market in Mongolia, the MSE, a state-owned joint stock company, was registered with the FRC as an SRO in 2015. As of 2019, the MSE had 52 securities firms as trading members.

As an SRO, the MSE sets and enforces listing rules, trading regulations, and disclosure obligations in addition to oversight and surveillance of its members. These rules and regulations set by the MSE are then authorized by the FRC.

The MSE operates a number of securities exchange markets, including the exchange-traded LCY government bond market and publicly offered corporate bond market. In addition, the MSE promotes investor education to retail investors through its beginner investment classes and issues certificates to the participants.

The functions and responsibilities of the MSE as an SRO include the following:

(i)   submit proposals to state organizations in relation to the improvement of securities market legislation; vote on draft laws, rules, and regulations developed by them;

(ii)   conduct professional training and retraining;

(iii)   adopt common rules, ethical standards, and recommendations of the members as presented by the FRC; ensure implementation and resolve complaints and disputes regarding the ethics of its members;

(iv)   request and receive information from its member organizations except for information that is prohibited by law;

(v)   research and analyze the activities of its members, assign ratings, and make them publicly available;

(vi)   review the activities of its members within the scope established by its rules and regulations, take responsibility to resolve violations, propose to the FRC proposals to suspend or revoke the member's license

depending on the magnitude of the violation, and report the violation to
the relevant organization;
(vii)   protect the legitimate interests of its members; and
(viii) take measures to reduce the risks of members' professional activities.

b.   Mongolian Association of Securities Dealers

The MASD is an industry organization established in 1995. It received its SRO status
in 2015 with the amendment of the Securities Market Law.

The MASD offers two different types of memberships: professional and partnering
members. Professional members consist of licensed securities companies; securities
clearing, settlement, and depository companies; securities trading companies; and
investment management companies. Partnering members consists of securities
nominee services companies, custodial services companies, investment funds, credit
rating agencies, and licensed advisory companies. As of 2019, the MASD had 51
members including 49 professional members and 2 partnering members. The
professional members include 44 securities companies, 3 asset management
companies, the MCSD, and the MSCH. The partnering members include local
custodian banks.

The association facilitates relations among market participants and represents its
members' interests with the regulators and the public. In addition, the MASD conducts
professional training and the certification of professionals. As part of its duties, the
MASD promotes fair business practices and investor protection, and enforces self-
regulatory measures such as administration of disciplinary measures to member
companies and employees failing to comply with the regulations.

2.   Market Participant Organizations

According to the Securities Market Law, a participant in the securities market is
defined as a securities issuer, a regulated entity, or an investor. A regulated entity is
defined as a legal entity licensed to engage in the following regulated activities set out
in Article 24.1 of the law:

(i)   securities brokering,
(ii)   securities dealing,
(iii)   securities investment advisory services,
(iv)   securities nominee services,
(v)   underwriting,
(vi)   registration of securities ownership rights,
(vii)   securities trading clearing,
(viii)   securities trading settlements,
(ix)   securities central depository services,
(x)   custodial services,
(xi)   securities trading,
(xii)   investment fund activities,
(xiii)   investment management activities,
(xiv)   credit rating services,
(xv)   providing legal advice to participants in the securities market,
(xvi)   providing property valuations and appraisal services for participants
         in the securities market,
(xvii)   providing auditing services for participants in the securities market, and
(xviii) such other activities as may be set down by the FRC.

The activities specified in Articles 24.1.1–14 and 24.1.18 of the Securities Market Law
can only be undertaken based on a license issued by the FRC. The activities specified

in Articles 24.1.15–17 of the law can be undertaken by a legal entity authorized to undertake the activity on the basis of having fulfilled the conditions and requirements set down by, and having registered with, the FRC.

The name of a regulated entity undertaking the activities specified in Articles 24.1.1–14 of the law is required to have a special designation after its company name, "*unet tsaasnii*" (securities company), or the abbreviation "UTsK," as required by law, except for stock exchanges, legal entities licensed to engage in securities central depository activities, and banks.

I.   Approval, Licensing, and Accreditation of Market Participants

1.   Market Participation as Securities Firms and Securities Representatives

According to the Securities Market Law, a regulated entity is defined as a participant in the securities market. A regulated entity is defined as a legal entity licensed to engage in the regulated activities set out in Article 24.1.

The list of activities specified in Article 24.2 of the Securities Market Law that can only be undertaken on the basis of a license issued by the FRC is as follows:

(i)   securities brokering,
(ii)   securities dealing,
(iii) securities investment advisory services,
(iv)   securities nominee services,
(v)   underwriting,
(vi)   registration of securities ownership rights,
(vii) securities trading clearing,
(viii) securities trading settlements,
(ix)   securities central depository services,
(x)   custodial services,
(xi)   securities trading,
(xii) investment fund activities,
(xiii) investment management activities, and
(xiv) credit rating services.

The law requires that the name of these regulated entities, include a special designation after its company name, which is *unet tsaasnii* (securities company), or the abbreviation UTsK. This is not a requirement for stock exchanges, legal entities licensed to engage in securities central depository activities, and banks.

The licensing of capital market participants is regulated under the FRC Regulation on Licensing Regulated Entities of Capital Market, amended as per FRC Decree No. 4, dated 9 January 2019.

As per Article 24.4 of the Securities Market Law, a license to undertake the credit rating activity shall be issued by the FRC in consultation with the BOM.

2.   Market Participation as Accredited or Registered Service Provider

According to Article 24.3 of the Securities Market Law, the following services can be undertaken by a legal entity authorized to undertake the concerned activity on the basis of having fulfilled the conditions and requirements set down by, and having registered with, the FRC:

(i)   legal advice to participants in the securities market,
(ii)   property valuations and appraisal services for participants in the securities market, and
(iii)   auditing services for participants in the securities market.

Registration of these capital market participants is regulated under the FRC Regulation on Licensing Regulated Entities of Capital Market, approved as per FRC Decree No. 4, dated 9 January 2019.

These service providers are independent advisors required to be hired by the issuer for the purposes of a public offer of securities in the Mongolian capital market, as required by the Securities Market Law and related regulations.

3.   Market Participants with Banking License

The BOM regulates the banking sector and issues banking licenses in accordance with the Banking Law (amended 18 January 2010), while NBFI activities such as factoring, underwriting, investment advisory services, and custodian and trust services are required to be licensed by the FRC.

According to Article 6.1 of the Banking Law, banks obtain licenses from the BOM to conduct the following activities:

(i)   accepting deposits;
(ii)   disbursing loans;
(iii)   payments and settlement services;
(iv)   providing payment guarantees and warranties to third parties on its own behalf;
(v)   purchasing, selling, and accepting and placing deposits in a foreign currency;
(vi)   purchasing, selling, and accepting and placing safety deposits of precious metals and stones;
(vii)   receiving valuables into custody;
(viii)   conducting foreign remittance services;
(ix)   issuing, buying, and selling securities;
(x)   dealing in financial leasing transactions;
(xi)   selling and buying loan portfolios and other financial instruments; and
(xii)   other financial transactions and services permitted by the laws and regulations and authorized by the BOM.

Issuing regular banking licenses is regulated under the BOM Regulation on License to Establish Bank (Decree No. A-82, dated 22 March 2019) and issuing additional licenses is regulated under the BOM Regulation on License to Conduct Banking Activities (Decree No. A-82, dated 22 March 2019). Activities (ii), (iii), (v), (vii), (viii), and (x) listed above are allowed under the regular banking license, while the rest require additional licenses. To obtain additional licenses, a bank must be compliant with prudential ratios for the last 6 consecutive months and have received a "good" evaluation on the latest onsite inspection of the BOM (Article 2.1.1 of the Regulation on License to Conduct Banking Activities).

As per Article 6.2 of the Banking Law, banks must obtain licenses to conduct the following activities from the FRC:

(i)   financial and investment advisory services,
(ii)   trust services,
(iii)   insurance brokerage,
(iv)   underwriting,
(v)   custodian, and
(vi)   factoring services.

The FRC is required by law to seek the BOM's consent prior to issuing a license for the above financial services to other members of a bank conglomerate.

J.   Stock Exchange Rules Related to Listing, Disclosure, and Trading of Debt Securities

1.   Debt Securities Listing Rules

a.   Mongolian Stock Exchange

The MSE lists publicly offered debt securities under its Listing Rules approved as per CEO Order No. 2018/01, dated 25 January 2018. The Listing Rules consist of 11 chapters and 26 articles covering the following regulations on the listing of shares and debt securities:

(i)   General provisions

(ii)   Listing securities for an initial public offering
        This chapter covers the preparation phase of listing (signing with an underwriting company, legal advisor, appraiser, or auditor and what these companies' reports shall include); application for listing (what documents to submit and which parties should sign the prospectus); and the contents and forms of the prospectus.

(iii)   Secondary listing of securities by foreign-exchange-listed issuers
        This chapter covers general requirements for foreign-exchange-listed nonresident issuers, applications for listing, and exemptions from certain ongoing obligations.

(iv)   Decision to list or refusal to list
        This chapter covers how many days the MSE will review the documents following submission, the conditions to refuse, and the listing and methods of securities listing. The MSE Listing Rules named six methods of listing: (a) current owner offering his or her shares; (b) private placement; (c) rights offering; (d) public offering; (e) conversion of retained earnings, paid-in capital, dividends, reserves and debts to equity; and (f) offering securities following merger and acquisition deals. Debt securities issued or fully guaranteed by the government shall be listed and traded on the MSE as per the approval from the MOF. Chapter III has the details.

(v)   Listing board and its criteria
        This chapter covers MSE's criteria to list debt securities and stocks and waivers and exemptions from listing criteria. Details in Chapter III.

(vi)   Amendments to listing

This chapter covers issuance of additional shares for private placement, secondary public offering, restructuring (mergers and acquisition) of the issuer and amending the listing, stock split and reverse-split, and updating classification of listing boards.

(vii)   Ongoing obligations of issuer

Key ongoing obligations include continuing to comply with the listing criteria; financial reporting under the IFRS; and transparency and compliance with relevant laws, regulations, and corporate governance principles.

(viii) Fees for issuers

Issuers shall pay an application review fee, an initial listing fee, and an annual listing fee. This chapter also covers payment frequencies and exemption criteria.

(ix)   Delisting the securities

This chapter covers which documents to submit in case of delisting and circumstances to delist securities.

(x)   Liabilities

This chapter covers consequences of violating the rules of the MSE.

(xi)   Miscellaneous

This chapter covers resolution of dispute and surveillance of the MSE.

Debt securities specific requirements are outlined in Article 14 of the Listing Rules. However, the MSE Listing Rules are not applicable to debt instruments issued in a foreign currency, debt instruments issued by foreign issuer, or debt instruments previously issued on a foreign (nonresident) exchange, as per Article 9.3.

The listing of investment trust units, asset-backed securities, depository receipts, and other derivative financial instruments shall not be regulated by the MSE Listing Rules and shall be governed by their respective regulations.

b.   Mongol Securities Exchange

The MSX lists publicly offered debt securities under its Listing Rules approved as per Board Order No. 16, dated 24 May 2018. The MSX Listing Rules consist of 22 chapters and 22 articles covering the following regulations on the listing of shares and debt securities:

(i)   General provisions

This chapter covers general provisions, a glossary of terms, general guidance, submission of information and documents, use of digital information, definition of market participants, guidelines on preparing information and documents, and conflicts of interest.

(ii)   Rights, roles, and activities of the listing unit, chief executive officer, listing committee, and board of directors

This chapter covers general provisions, acceptance and resolution of applications, procedures on imposing disciplinary actions, roles of the board and board meetings, principles of justice, and activities of the listing unit.

(iii)   Monitoring

This chapter covers general provisions, monitoring by the listing committee and the board, timeline for requesting review of decisions, statement of the monitoring meeting, monitoring meeting, request for justification of the decision, and fees.

(iv)   Listing methods
This chapter covers general provisions, offering by way of taking orders, and offering by selling own securities to company shareholders.

(v)   Requirements for securities and issuers
This chapter covers general provisions, prerequisites, profitability requirements, market capitalization and revenue and cashflow requirements, new applicants, underwriters, distribution of securities, persons belonging and not belonging to the public, and listing on the emerging board.

(vi)   Underwriter and market maker
This chapter covers general provisions, contracting the underwriter, duties of new applicants to the underwriter, independence of the underwriter, additional underwriter, roles of the underwriter, statement of the underwriter, termination of the underwriter's duties, contracting the market maker, duties of the market maker to the exchange, termination of the market maker's duties, and other provisions.

(vii)   Listing application and its requirements
This chapter covers general provisions, exemption from listing requirements, submission and review of the listing application, preliminary consultation on the final draft of the registration document, submitting the final draft of the registration document with supporting documentation, review and resolution of the exchange, registration of the securities to the FRC, printing and formalizing of the registration document, introducing the registration document to the public, activities before public offer, requirements on documents, and securities issued by the listed issuer.[12]

(viii)   Registration document
This chapter covers general provisions, contents of the registration document, responsibilities, amending the registration document, language, pictures and graphics, profit forecast, and notices.

(ix)   Opinion of professional accountant and estimated financial information
This chapter covers general provisions, requirements for a professional accountant, additional information to be included in the registration document, accounting standards and applicable legislations, adjustments, amendments to the opinion of a professional accountant, foreign issuers, estimated financial information, and other provisions.

(x)   Property valuation
This chapter covers general provisions, requirements for applicants, property valuation report, property appraiser, and other provisions.

(xi)   Methods of public distribution of registration document
This chapter covers general provisions, publicizing the registration document, providing information to the public after the securities offering, and introducing the registration document in print and digital formats.

(xii)   Restrictions on placing orders and purchase of securities
This chapter covers general provisions, types of restrictions, and other provisions.

---

[12] The registration document refers to the securities prospectus.

(xiii)   Authorized representative, board members, board committees, and general secretariat of the listed issuer

This chapter covers the authorized representative, board members of the listed issuer, audit committee, remuneration committee, and general secretariat.

(xiv)   Trading halt and delisting of securities

This chapter covers a temporary trading halt, suspension of securities, and delisting at the request of the issuer.

(xv)   Registration methods (debt instruments)

This chapter covers methods of offering by way of placing orders and debt instrument owners offering to sell their debt instruments.

(xvi)   Requirements for listing (debt instruments)

This chapter covers general provisions, prerequisites, and stability.

(xvii)   Listing application and its requirements (debt instruments)

This chapter covers general provisions and requirements for registration documents.

(xviii)   Registration document (debt instruments)

This chapter covers general provisions, contents, responsibilities, language, pictures and graphs, informing the public of the registration document, presenting the registration document in print and digital format, informing the public on the debt instrument, and notices.

(xix)   Listing agreement (debt instruments)

This chapter covers general provisions and communication with the exchange.

(xx)   Debt instruments of government, municipal, and city governors

This chapter covers debt instruments, listing requirements, and the registration document.

(xxi)   Guarantor and guaranteed securities

This chapter covers general provisions on the guarantor and guaranteed securities.

(xxii)   Double listing

This chapter covers general provisions, listing requirements, the application for listing, the registration document, investor protection, the listing agreement, and other provisions.

Although the MSX Listing Rules have specific clauses on debt instruments, they lack provisions on information disclosure. The MSX is a privately held regulated securities exchange that acquired its license in 2015. It had its first listing in 2017 and had one company listed and one publicly offered corporate debt securities listed as of 2019.

2.   Debt Securities Related Disclosure Requirements

a.   Mongolian Stock Exchange

The MSE has no specialized rules and regulations on disclosure requirements dedicated specifically for debt securities issuers. All types of security issuers in the public market are required to follow the same rules and guidelines.

As per Article 21 of the MSE Listing Rules, listed companies have an obligation to disclose information that may have an impact on the price and trading activities of its securities:[13]

(i) The issuer shall have a dedicated securities specialist in charge of disseminating information pertaining to the securities to the public and to ensure implementation of the duties to shareholders and authorized bodies.[14]

(ii) The issuer shall inform the public and the exchange about its operations, financial situation, and any information that may have an impact on the price and trading activities of the securities as per the law and the relevant regulations from the FRC.[15] In the case of a foreign-listed issuer, the issuer shall follow Article 7.1 for publishing information.[16]

Detailed rules on what information and documents should be submitted and when these documents should be uploaded are stated in the MSE Guidelines on Submitting Information Electronically for Listed Companies.

b.   Mongol Securities Exchange

According to Article 1.19 of the MSX Listing Rules, the issuer is required to submit all types of information the exchange deems necessary to protect investor interests or to ensure normal market operation in a timely manner. There are no specific rules or guidelines dedicated to information disclosure at the MSX at present.

3.   Debt Securities Trading Rules and Market Conventions

a.   Mongolian Stock Exchange

Stocks, corporate debt securities, and government bonds trading on the MSE are regulated by the MSE Guidelines on Trading Activities, Trading Rules for Secondary Market Trading, Primary Market Issuance Rules, and Guidelines on Primary Market Issuance of Government Securities for primary market issuance:

1) Guidelines on Trading Activities

The MSE Guidelines on Trading Activities, approved per CEO Decree No. 165, dated 17 October 2014, are dedicated to regulate daily trading sessions of the MSE, such as the times for pre-trading (9:25 a.m.–9:40 a.m.), opening auction call (9:40 a.m.–10:00 a.m.), regular trading (10:00 a.m.–1:00 p.m.), market close (1:00 p.m.–1:05 p.m.), and post-trading (1:05 p.m.–2:00 p.m.). As per the guidance, securities firms can participate in trading either physically at the MSE building or remotely. In practice, very few brokers trade physically at the MSE building.

2) Trading Rules for Secondary Market Trading

The MSE Trading Rules for Secondary Market Trading, approved per Board Resolution No. 2, dated 10 February 2012 (amended 13 December 2017), regulate the trading of all securities listed on the MSE.[17] The rules specify order

---

[13] Listed companies refers to companies with shares listed and traded on the MSE.

[14] A dedicated securities specialist refers to investor relations staff appointed by the company.

[15] Details of disclosure requirements set forth in the law and FRC regulations can be found in Chapter II.G of this bond market guide.

[16] A foreign-listed issuer may follow the laws, rules, and regulations of the country and exchange of primary listing when submitting any reports or information to the FRC and the MSE. All the information and documents provided to the foreign (nonresident) exchange and regulator shall be submitted simultaneously to the MSE with a Mongolian translation on a regular basis (where necessary, a brief summary of the information in Mongolian can be provided).

[17] An unofficial translation of the MSE Trading Rules is available at Mongolian Stock Exchange. 2017. Trading Rules. http://mse.mn/uploads/laws/MSE%20Trading%20Rules%20ENG.pdf.

types, block trades, all-or-none trades, order amendments and cancellations, closing price calculation, trading halts, fees, and more. As there are no specifications on corporate debt securities trading, this type of trading takes place in the same manner as all other securities traded on the MSE.

3) Primary Market Issuance Rules

The MSE Primary Market Issuance Rules, approved as per Board Resolution No. 15, dated 26 October 2018, detail several types of primary market issuance methods, including book-building offering, auction and fixed price offering, as well as allocation methods.

This regulation does not specify primary market issuance rules of corporate debt securities, such as requirements on par values and the allocation of oversubscribed issuance. In practice, publicly offered corporate debt securities are generally priced at par value of MNT100,000 or less to encourage more retail investors to enter the market. In the case of oversubscription, the orders are allocated proportionally.

4) Guidelines on Primary Market Issuance of Government Securities

The MSE Guidelines on Primary Market Issuance of Government Securities, approved as per CEO Decree No. A/115, dated 4 July 2017, detail trading types, participants, and the settlement of government bonds. As mentioned previously, while government bond off-exchange issuance takes place via BOM among commercial banks (banks can take orders from other investors as non-direct participants), government bond exchange issuance takes place via the MSE by any investor through a brokerage firm, as per the 2014 Government Regulation on Issuance and Trading of Government Securities.

Based on the issuers' (MOF) request to list government securities, the Chief Executive Officer (CEO) of the MSE resolves to list and issue government bonds in the primary market. This resolution is then sent to the MCSD to register the government bonds. After the primary market issuance sessions, the MSE sends the order blotter to the MOF to allocate the orders.

MSE member firms are the only entities allowed to participate in the trading. Trading participants are required to enter investors' orders every Tuesday from 10:00 a.m. to 11:30 a.m. Investors are required to prefund their trading accounts at the MSCH before the trading takes place.

Primary offering methods of government bonds include noncompetitive bidding and competitive bidding. If an issuance is noncompetitive, the interest rate is predefined and trading participants are not allowed to enter orders below or above the predefined rate. There have been only three instances of government bonds being offered by a competitive bidding method on the MSE. All of these occurred prior to October 2017 when the MOF temporarily halted LCY government bond issuance under the IMF bailout program. Generally, exchange issuance of government bonds was offered via a noncompetitive bidding method and followed pricing determined among the banks in the off-exchange issuance of government bonds.

However, with the newly approved 2019 Government Regulation on Primary and Secondary Market Operations of Domestic Government Securities, which removed the distinction between exchange issuance and off-exchange issuance of government bonds, the current MSE guidelines might be amended once the government starts issuing bonds again.

b.   Mongol Securities Exchange

Securities trading on the MSX is regulated by the MSX Trading Rules and Regulation on Clearing Activities.

1)   Trading Rules

The MSX Trading Rules, approved as per Board Decree No. 14, dated 16 May 2018, are dedicated to regulating the daily trading sessions of the MSX. The rules outline the roles and responsibilities of market participants, trading schedules, trading boards, trading methods, trading information, market monitoring, trading fees, and dispute resolution.

2)   Regulation on Clearing Activities

The MSX Regulation on Clearing Activities, approved as per Board Decree No. 14, dated 16 May 2018, is dedicated to regulating the clearing activities of the MSX under the securities clearing license granted by the FRC. The regulation outlines the roles and responsibilities of market participants and clearing members with regard to clearing activities, registration, monitoring of clearing members, clearing accounts, collaterals, fees, clearing infrastructure, and dispute resolution.

K.   Market Entry Requirements (Nonresidents)

1.   Nonresident Issuer Entry Requirements

Under the Securities Market Law and FRC regulations, foreign-exchange-listed nonresident issuers that are regulated by the International Organization of Securities Commissions member regulator can issue securities in Mongolia with the approval of the FRC.

In such cases, it is not considered that the company is conducting business within Mongolian territory, according to the law. However, there is no specific clause on whether an entity registered but not listed in a foreign jurisdiction is allowed to publicly offer its securities in the Mongolian market, and there has been no such case to date.

As per the Securities Market Law, the FRC has approved the Temporary Regulation on Registering Securities Offered in Mongolia by a Foreign Exchange Listed Entity and Securities Offered in a Foreign Country by a Mongolian Exchange Listed Entity, on 24 November 2017.

This allows fast-tracking of securities issuances by foreign issuers on a preapproved list of foreign (nonresident) exchanges by the FRC. The regulatory process is simpler because the listing request is not required to have a business and asset valuation report or an underwriter's opinion. It is still required to have a legal opinion by a licensed entity and an audited financial report. The documents are required to be translated into Mongolian, but only the original language version has legal authority and is required to be submitted as well.

Under this regulation, a foreign-exchange-listed nonresident issuer can submit its request for a securities listing to the FRC and the MSE at the same time and is only allowed to offer its securities on the public offering market after it has been approved by the FRC and been registered at the FRC and the MCSD.

Although there was one case of an equity dual-listing of nonresident listed securities in 2018, no publicly offered corporate debt securities from a nonresident issuer have been issued to date, as this regulation was developed with an equity listing in mind. It is unclear whether it can be applied to a public offering of debt securities.

More specifically, this regulation is primarily for equity issuances, as Article 9.3 of the MSE Listing Rules states that the listing rules are not applicable to the debt securities issued by a foreign-listed issuer, debt securities denominated in foreign currency, and debt securities previously issued on a foreign (nonresident) exchange.

2.   Foreign Investor Entry Requirements

The Securities Market Law makes no specific distinction between foreign investors and domestic investors. However, all investors participating in the Mongolian public market are required to have a trading account at an FRC-licensed securities brokerage firm, a domestic bank account, and an account at the MCSD. To open these accounts, an investor is required to submit the documents in writing. For foreign companies, additional documentation and fees are needed to open these accounts and the original documents are required to be physically submitted. However, investors can open an omnibus account with a securities firm or a custodian, which would simplify some of these procedures.

L.   Market Exit Requirements (Nonresidents)

1.   Nonresident Issuer Exit Requirements

There are no specific exit requirements for nonresident issuers in the Mongolian market, as foreign and domestic issuers are both treated the same under the current legislation.

2.   Foreign Investor Exit Requirements

The Securities Market Law has no specific distinction on foreign investors and domestic investors. All investors participating in the Mongolian public market are required to have a trading account at an FRC-licensed securities brokerage firm and an account at the MCSD. To withdraw funds from their own account at the MCSD, investors are required to submit a written request and the original documents are required to be physically submitted.

There are no limitations on currency exchange or any restrictions on the transfer of funds out of Mongolian bank accounts in the relevant laws and regulations.

M.   Regulations and Limitations Relevant for Nonresidents

1.   Taxation of Nonresidents

According to the General Taxation Law (amended 22 March 2019), dividends, interest, and rental income are subject to Mongolian personal income tax at the flat rate of 10% for residents and 20% withholding tax for the Mongolian-sourced income of nonresidents, unless the term is reduced pursuant to an applicable tax treaty.

For the capital gains tax, the same 10% rate applies in principle, but market practice needs to be referred to the local custodian for confirmation.

For the corporate income tax, up to MNT6 billion in taxable income is taxed at a rate of 10%, while income in excess of MNT6 billion is taxed at 25%.

Government bonds and debt instruments issued by the Development Bank of Mongolia are exempt from income tax under the current tax legislation. In addition, under the revised Corporate Income Tax Law and Personal Income Tax Law (effective 1 January 2020), interest income earned from publicly offered corporate debt securities are subject to a 5% income tax instead of 10%. Capital gains from the trading of publicly offered corporate debt securities are subject to the standard tax rate of 10% for individuals and either 10% or 25% for corporates.

2.   Currency Exchange Controls

According to Article 4 of the Law on the Bank of Mongolia, the main objective of the BOM is to ensure stability of the national currency, the togrog. As its main objective per the law, the BOM shall maintain the stability of the financial market and banking system to support the balanced development of the national economy.

Although Mongolia has a floating foreign currency exchange rate regime, during times of unstable market conditions, the central bank sometimes intervenes in the foreign currency market through the local banks to maintain a steady exchange rate, within the scope of its main objective. There are no foreign currency exchange controls restricting investment and trade either in or out of the Mongolia.

However, according to Article 4 of the Law On Conducting Settlements In National Currency (enacted 9 July 2009), the price of goods, work, and services shall be expressed and settlement shall be conducted only in togrog within the territory of Mongolia. It is prohibited to set prices, carry out settlements, and run advertisements in foreign currencies or settlement units without official BOM approval, except for bank and NBFI loans, deposits, and related services.

Generally, currency hedging is available to local banks through long-term currency swap agreements with the BOM. While foreign investors or lenders can access this hedging mechanism through local banks, the cost of hedging is very high in general.

3.   Bank Accounts in Domestic or Foreign Currency

A foreigner or a foreign entity is not restricted from opening a bank account in any local bank in Mongolia, and there are no limitations on transferring of funds in or out of Mongolia.

The Government of Mongolia employs exceptionally liberal policies for controlling foreign exchange for investment remittances. Although there is no difficulty in exchanging foreign currencies from the local banks, there are times when limits are set by the local banks based on the availability of foreign currency in the local market place.

4.   Borrowing and Lending

Borrowing and lending activities by nonresident entities are subject to the same regulations that are applicable to residents.

Commercial banking licenses are regulated by the BOM under the Central Bank Law (enacted 3 September 1996). NBFI licenses are regulated by the FRC under the Law on Legal Status of the Financial Regulatory Commission (enacted 17 November 2005).

Financial leasing activities are regulated by the Financial Leasing Law (enacted 22 June 2006) and the Civil Law (enacted 10 January 2002) of Mongolia.[18]

5.   Nonresident Transaction Requirements at Banks

In regard to domestic transactions, the Parliament of Mongolia enacted the Law on Settling Payments in National Currency in 2009, mandating that prices of goods, work, and services shall be expressed and settlement shall be conducted only in the national currency within the territory of Mongolia. As a result, all domestic transactions must be conducted in the togrog, except for those entities allowed specific waivers as determined by the BOM and the FRC.

The Government of Mongolia allows funds to flow easily in and out of the domestic economy with one exception. Foreign-held, interest-bearing United States dollar (USD) accounts are subject to a 20% withholding tax unless the term is reduced pursuant to an applicable tax treaty. Typically, the local bank retains 20% of these interest payments sent abroad and remits to the Tax Authority of Mongolia.

N.   Regulations on Credit Rating Agencies

There are no credit rating agencies (CRAs) present in Mongolia. A handful of Mongolian conglomerates—such as the Mongolian Mining Corporation, Tavan Bogd Group, and MIK Holding JSC—have appointed international CRAs before issuing USD-denominated debt securities in international capital markets.

As per Article 24.1 of the Securities Market Law, a CRA is a regulated entity required to obtain a license from the FRC. Under Article 50.4 of the Securities Market Law, the FRC approved the Regulation on Credit Rating Activities per Decree No. 529, dated 18 December 2013. The regulation covers the following areas on CRA activities:

a)   Obtaining a License

Shareholders of CRAs are required to be a (i) domestic or international financial firm, (ii) commercial bank, (iii) domestic legal entity with sales revenue above MNT1 billion, or (iv) an international CRA with at least 3 years of credit rating experience. The minimum share capital requirement is MNT100 million. CRAs are required to have a minimum of two analysts, one internal control officer, and a rating committee with a minimum of five members. Credit rating licenses are given indefinitely.

b)   Operations of a Credit Rating Agency

CRAs are required to follow the International Organization of Securities Commissions' CRA Code and the FRC's Code of Conduct in its everyday activities. The regulation also addresses clauses required to be in a contract signed between the CRA and the client. CRAs are required to monitor and analyze clients regularly.

c)   Obligations of a Credit Rating Agency

CRAs are required to submit operational reports on a semiannual basis and financial statements on a quarterly basis to the FRC. Resolutions and reports of any new or amended credit ratings are required to be reported to the FRC within 5 days of release. The salary and compensation of rating committee members

---

[18] An unofficial translation of the Civil Law (Civil Code) of Mongolia can be found at https://www.ebrd.com/downloads/legal/securities/mongcc.pdf.

and analysts are required to be transparent and any amendments made are required to be reported to the FRC. CRAs are required to keep annual financial statements, annual audit reports, credit rating contracts with clients, documents received from clients, client information, credit rating reports, minutes of rating committee meetings, and payment receipts for at least 5 years. CRAs are prohibited to receive payments on any services apart from a credit rating.

d)   Limitations on a Credit Rating Agency

If a shareholder of a CRA is a lending business, its management and employees are prohibited from being a manager or employee of the CRA, or of its rating committee. CRAs are prohibited from offering credit rating services on their (i) own securities, (ii) related parties, (iii) shareholders, (iv) shareholders' lenders, and (v) shareholders' related parties.

e)   Financial Regulatory Commission Supervision of Credit Rating Agencies

The FRC will conduct inspections on (i) maintaining the aforementioned documents, (ii) implementation of relevant laws and regulations, and (iii) complaints received from investors, clients, or others. The FRC is required to notify CRAs at least 10 calendar days before inspection. The FRC will take suitable actions based on the inspection report.

f)   Suspending, Reinstating, and Revoking a Credit Rating License

The FRC will suspend a credit rating license if (i) situations stated in Article 29.1 of the Securities Market Law and Article 13.1 of Special Licenses Law occur, (ii) financial statements are not submitted 2 quarters in a row, (iii) any required documents are not submitted on time, (iv) any regulatory fees are not paid on time, and (v) the CRA did not abide by the Regulation on Credit Rating Activities.

The FRC will revoke a credit rating license if (i) situations stated in Article 30.1 of the Securities Market Law and Article 14.1 of Special Licenses Law occur; (ii) no actions were taken during the suspension period; (iii) the CRA inflicted serious damage on investors, clients, and the capital market; (iv) the CRA made morally hazardous mistakes; (v) the CRA is liquidated and/or bankrupt; and (vi) the CRA did not oblige with the Regulation on Credit Rating Activities. Clients of a CRA with a revoked license should choose another CRA.

g)   Obtaining Approval to Change Shareholder Structure, Amend Company Name, Appoint and Discharge Chief Executive Officer, and Open a Branch

CRAs are required to receive approval from the FRC when (i) changing shareholder structure, (ii) changing a company name, (iii) appointing and discharging the CEO, and (iv) opening a new branch.

O.   Regulations on Securities Pricing Agencies

At present, Mongolia does not have a dedicated debt instruments or securities pricing agency, and there are no related regulations in place.

III

Characteristics of the Mongolian Bond Market

The Mongolian bond market is in its early stages of development, and privately placed corporate debt instruments currently dominate the market in the absence of LCY government bond issuances. Exchange-listed corporate debt securities are not common due to time-consuming issuance procedures. It is desirable to establish a proper regulatory framework for private placement of corporate bonds, or create an exempt regime of public offering to support timely corporate bond issuance.

The detailed characteristics of the bond market in Mongolia are described in this chapter.

A.   Definition of Securities

Though the term "bond" is commonly used in the market, the Securities Market Law does not specifically refer to a bond. Under the law, debt instruments are defined as one type of securities. Thus, the legal terminology for bond is "debt instrument."

Government bonds are also termed "government securities" or "government debt securities" in the Debt Management Law. As such, the terms debt instrument and debt securities are used primarily in this guide, except when the term "bond" is preferred. There are no terms such as short-term notes, commercial paper, or short-term bills in the regulations.[19]

Privately placed corporate debt instruments (referred to as closed) are beyond the scope of the Securities Market Law; hence, the Company Law is the only relevant law. The Securities Market Law defines and regulates securities in general, while privately placed corporate debt instruments are generally issued in practice with a purchase agreement between the issuer, underwriter, and investors. These privately placed debt instruments would not be considered securities under the current regulations.

However, if the privately placed corporate debt instruments are registered at a securities depository entity (either the MCSD or custodian) that is regulated by the FRC, then the debt instruments can be deemed as securities under the Securities Market Law. As per the law, registration at a depository entity is considered legal proof of ownership of the securities.

---

[19] In many financial markets around the world, money market refers to the short-term financial market that lends and borrows short-term funds with a term of less than 1 year. Within the money market is an interbank money market where only financial institutions can participate, and an open money market where general business corporations can also participate. In the wholesale money market, with its large denomination, a negotiable certificate of deposit is issued by bank and commercial paper is issued by business corporations and financial institutions. The bond market, on the other hand, is a capital market with debt instruments that generally have a term of 1 year or more. However, in Mongolia, the distinction between the money market and the bond market is not necessarily clear. In some markets, commercial paper is recognized as a short-term corporate debt instrument, but in many markets commercial paper is often treated as a privately placed instrument, usually due to its short-term and wholesale nature.

Although these privately placed corporate debt instruments legally do not constitute securities, as they are loan agreements, based on current market practice, they are considered corporate bonds in the Mongolian domestic market and tend to be marketed as bonds.

Legally, pursuant to Articles 4 and 5 of the Securities Market Law, securities are defined as follows:

(i)   shares of joint stock company;
(ii)   corporate debt instruments;
(iii)   shares or unit rights in an investment fund;
(iv)   depositary receipts;
(v)   asset-backed securities;
(vi)   rights to purchase a certain number of shares or debt instruments that are offered by a securities issuer to an investor, within a certain period of time and at an agreed price (warrants);
(vii) derivative financial instruments specified in this law; and
(viii) such other financial instruments as may be deemed by the FRC to be securities in accordance with this law.

Debt instruments in the law are defined as securities evidencing an obligation to repay principal and interest to holders of the same, either in cash or in kind in the form of certain property or property rights at the expiry of the term, or any similar securities, as per Article 4.1.9 of the law.

Government securities are defined in Article 4.1.19 of the Debt Management Law as debt securities issued in accordance with the purpose and procedures provided by this law. Article 12.1 of the Debt Management Law defines the purpose of issuing debt securities as follows:

(i)   financing budget deficits,
(ii)   financing seasonal shortfalls in budget revenues,
(iii)   supporting the domestic government securities market,
(iv)   debt refinancing,
(v)   financing national investment programs,
(vi)   increasing the BOM's net foreign currency reserves to support the national balance of payments, and
(vii) recapitalizing banks by the state in accordance with the Banking Sector Stability Law.

B.   Types of Bonds

The Mongolian bond market features a number of debt instruments from both government and corporate issuers. Debt instruments may be publicly offered (referred to as open) or privately placed (referred to as closed). All publicly offered debt instruments are required to be registered with the FRC, deposited at the MCSD, traded on an exchange, and transferred electronically.

This section reviews the different types of debt instruments available in the market.

1.   Debt Securities Issued by Public Entities

Prior to the temporary halt of government bond issuance in 2017, the MOF issued government bonds as per the Regulation on Issuance and Trading of Government Securities. Under this previous regulation, government bonds were issued off-exchange and through exchange issuance methods.[20] The off-exchange issuance was conducted through the BOM's interbank over-the-counter (OTC) market, while the exchange issuance was conducted through the MSE. Registration and transfer of ownership were made at the MCSD. The BOM handled the cash settlement process of government bonds. All government bonds were issued in scripless form as electronic records in the MCSD book-entry system.

The newly approved 2019 Government Regulation on Primary and Secondary Market Operations of Domestic Government Securities has removed the distinction of exchange issuance and off-exchange issuance of government bonds. Under this new regulation, the MOF is to choose the issuance venue once the government bond issuance restarts, although the application of this regulation in practice has yet to be seen.

There is no clear distinction for government bonds in terms of maturity length in the related regulations, and all government bonds are termed and categorized in the same manner. Additionally, there are no terms such as "Treasury bills" in the regulations.

a.   Government Bonds

Government bonds (referred to as government securities) are issued by the MOF (referred to as an issuer) in accordance with the Debt Management Law for the purposes of financing budget deficits, financing seasonal shortfalls in budget revenues, supporting the domestic government securities market, debt refinancing, financing national investment programs, increasing the net foreign currency reserves of BOM to support the national balance of payments, and recapitalizing banks by the state in accordance with the Banking Sector Stability Law.

Government securities are not regulated by the Securities Market Law. The Securities Market Law was amended in 18 February 2015 to remove government and municipal bonds from the list of securities regulated by the law.

According to the Debt Management Law, the total amount of government bonds to be issued each fiscal year is required to be included in the state budget prepared by the MOF and approved by the Parliament in accordance with the debt ceiling for that fiscal year. The issuance schedule is approved by the MOF, and the bonds are issued in a periodic manner.

Before the temporary issuance halt in 2017, government bonds were issued on a weekly basis for both exchange and off-exchange issuances. The issuance schedule was published quarterly by the MOF. The bonds had tenors of 3, 6, 9, 12, 24, 36, and 60 months; and were issued at a discount to par value through an auction bidding process. The bonds were registered at the MCSD in dematerialized form and prefunded and settled at T+1.

Government bonds are tax exempt from interest income taxes as per Article 16.1 of the Personal Income Tax Law and Article 18.1 of the Corporate Tax Law.

According to Article 8.12 of the 2019 Government Regulation on Primary and Secondary Market Operations of Domestic Government Securities, the government may issue short-term government securities that are repayable within the same fiscal year, by private placement to the BOM, for the purpose of financing seasonal budget shortfalls.

---

[20] Off-exchange refers to the interbank over-the-counter market. Exchange issuance refers to securities listed and traded on an exchange.

As of December 2019, a total of MNT1.4 trillion worth of government securities was outstanding at the MCSD. The weighted-average interest rate of outstanding government securities was 11.95%.

b.   Government-Guaranteed Bonds

Government-guaranteed securities are regulated by the Securities Market Law and the Debt Management Law. According to Article 10.15 of the Securities Market Law, publicly offered government-guaranteed securities can be exempt from producing a securities prospectus. Pursuant to the Debt Management Law, government guarantees are required to be made in accordance with the Debt Management Law and approved and monitored by the government.

Currently, there are no government-guaranteed bonds in the LCY bond market. Government-guaranteed bonds were issued by the Development Bank of Mongolia only in the international bond market. The Development Bank of Mongolia previously issued USD-denominated, government-guaranteed bonds, which were listed on the Singapore Exchange.

c.   Municipal Bonds

As per the 7 September 2016 amendment to the Debt Management Law, provinces and the capital city are not allowed to issue debt securities. Municipal bonds have never been issued in Mongolia.

2.   Corporate Debt Instruments

Corporate debt instruments are issued by joint stock companies, limited liability companies, and state-owned enterprises under the Securities Market Law and Company Law.

Corporate debt instruments can be publicly offered (referred to as open) or privately placed (referred to as closed). Publicly offered corporate debt instruments are regulated under the Securities Market Law and the FRC.

Corporate debt instruments are recognized as open securities if the number of investors exceeds 50.[21] If the number of investors is 50 or less, then debt instruments are regarded as closed securities per the Regulation on Securities Registration of the FRC.[22]

As the Mongolian LCY corporate bond market's development is in its early stage and with the lack of professional institutional investors in the market, retail investors are the primary participants in the domestic corporate bond market.

As of December 2019, there were no publicly offered corporate debt instruments listed on the exchanges.

a.   Denomination of Corporate Debt Instruments

The currency of most corporate debt instrument issuance in the domestic market is the togrog. However, there have been instances of privately placed corporate debt instruments denominated in USD. Although some publicly offered corporate debt securities on the MSE were denominated in USD in the past, it is no longer allowed to

---

[21] Open securities refer to publicly offered securities.
[22] Closed securities refer to privately placed securities.

list publicly offered foreign-currency-denominated corporate debt securities under the MSE Listing Rules.[23]

b.   Types of Corporate Debt Instruments

Publicly offered corporate debt instruments are regulated and required to go through a (i) registration process at the FRC and (ii) listing process at the exchange. Once these regulatory bodies approve the registration and listing of the debt securities, registration at the central depository is required to be eligible for trading on the exchange. These publicly offered corporate debt securities were electronically transferred and settled on T+1 through a prefunded settlement process. The FRC and the MSCH have completed the process of converting to a T+2 settlement cycle from the current prefunded settlement regime, and shifted to a delivery versus payment scheme starting from 31 March 2020.

Privately placed corporate debt instruments are outside the scope of the Securities Market Law and therefore are regulated by the Company Law. As the Securities Market Law regulates and defines securities in general, and privately placed corporate debt instruments are generally issued in practice with a purchase agreement between the issuer, the underwriter, and investors, these privately placed debt instruments are not deemed as securities under the current regulations.

However, if the privately placed corporate debt instruments are registered at a regulated securities depository entity (MCSD or a custodian) that is regulated by the FRC, then the debt instruments can be deemed as securities under the Securities Market Law. As per the law, registration at a depository entity is legal proof of ownership of the securities.

Corporate debt instruments issued on the Mongolian market typically have a term of 3, 6, 9, 12, or 18 months. The longest maturity recorded for publicly offered corporate debt instruments is 24 months. It is not common in the market to issue debt instruments with a maturity longer than 12 months as investors are not used to such long-term investments.

As a market practice, the par value of corporate debt instruments ranges between MNT100,000 and MNT1,000,000. Most publicly offered corporate debt securities, however, typically have a face value of MNT100,000 to attract more retail investors, while privately placed debt instruments tend to have a face value of MNT1,000,000.

There has been no unsecured corporate debt instrument issuance in the Mongolian bond market. In practice, corporate debt instruments are secured by either collateral or the guarantee of a third party. The majority of these corporate debt securities are typically collateralized by either real estate assets or shares of the company.

C.   Money Market Instruments

This section reviews the commonly available money market instruments in the Mongolian interbank market, aside from government bonds. The key money market instruments are government and central bank securities repurchase agreements (repos), central bank bills (CBBs), overnight lending, and interbank deposits.

In Mongolia, there is no open money market that general business corporations can participate in.

---

[23] Article 9.3 of the MSE Listing Rules states that the MSE Listing Rules are not applicable to debt securities denominated in a foreign currency or debt securities issued by a foreign-listed issuer.

Figure 3.1: Interbank Money Market Trading Volume

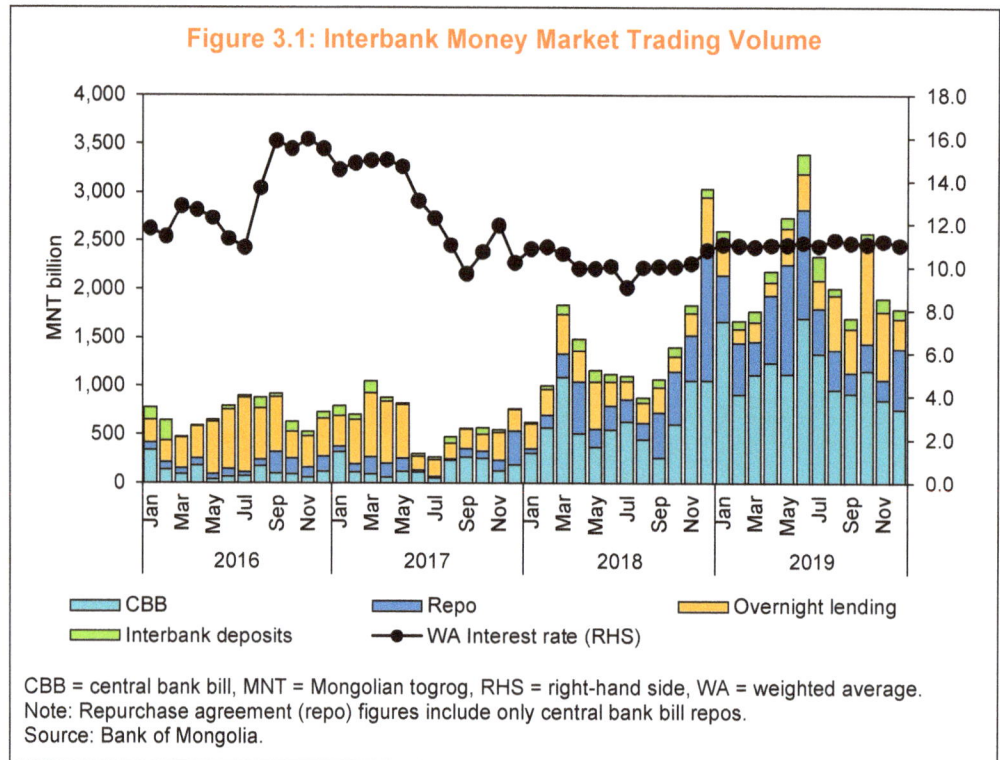

CBB = central bank bill, MNT = Mongolian togrog, RHS = right-hand side, WA = weighted average.
Note: Repurchase agreement (repo) figures include only central bank bill repos.
Source: Bank of Mongolia.

Interbank transactions follow the common legislation as there are no dedicated regulations for the interbank money market. However, each interbank money market instrument follows its own dedicated regulations developed by the BOM. Interbank transactions and settlements go through the BOM system.

Transaction volume at the interbank market has picked up since 2018 after the government temporarily halted government bond issuance in October 2017 as a result of the IMF EFF. In addition, the BOM decreased the frequency and increased the maturity of CBB issuance beginning in April 2018, resulting in more secondary market trading activity in the interbank market. In 2017, total transaction volume at the interbank market was MNT7.7 trillion; while in 2019, the volume had increased to MNT26.7 trillion (Figure 3.1).

The BOM has kept its policy rate steady at 11.0% since 27 November 2018, when it increased the policy rate by 100 basis points from 10.0%.

1.   Central Bank Bills

To achieve its monetary policy measures, the BOM issues CBBs to tap surplus liquidity in the market and affect short-term interest rates. By issuing CBBs, the BOM prevents surplus reserves and mitigates the volatility of short-term interest rates in the interbank market. Commercial banks can trade CBBs with the BOM and with each other on the interbank market.

CBB issuance and trading is regulated by the Law on the Bank of Mongolia and the Regulation on the Trading of Central Bank Bills. As per regulations, CBBs have the following terms:

(i)   As per Article 2.2 of the regulation, CBBs shall be issued through one of the following methods and the method of issuance shall be announced in the notification of the CBB:
   (a)   fixed-rate tender with or without preannounced volumes;
   (b)   variable-rate tender with interest rate bids being submitted within a certain interval; or
   (c)   variable-rate tender with upper limits on interest rate bids and without preannounced volumes, or variable-rate tender with limited volumes.
(ii) CBBs shall utilize book-entry issuance and have a maturity of up to 1 year. The face value of each CBB will be MNT1 million.

The BOM quotes the terms of CBBs in line with interbank market conditions and monetary policy as follows:

(i)   until April 2018, 1-week CBBs were traded three times a week with a fixed interest rate and in unlimited quantity;
(ii)   since April 2013, 4-week CBBs have been traded once a week with a fixed interest rate and in unlimited quantity;
(iii) until March 2013, 12-week CBBs were traded once every 2 weeks; and
(iv)   since November 2018, 28-week CBBs have been traded once every 2 weeks with upper limits on the interest rate and in a limited amount.

Fixed-rate CBBs are priced at par with the policy rate. For CBBs with an upper limit on the interest rate, the maximum possible bid rate is the policy rate +1% as per Decree No. A-173 of the Governor of the BOM.

As there has been no government bond issuance since October 2017, demand for CBBs has increased drastically. Although there was the risk of reduced interbank trading due to government bond issuance freeze, the BOM took appropriate actions and implemented policies to sustain interbank market activity. As of December 2019, the total outstanding balance of CBBs on commercial bank balance sheets was MNT4.7 trillion, up from MNT0.6 trillion in December 2016 (Figure 3.2).

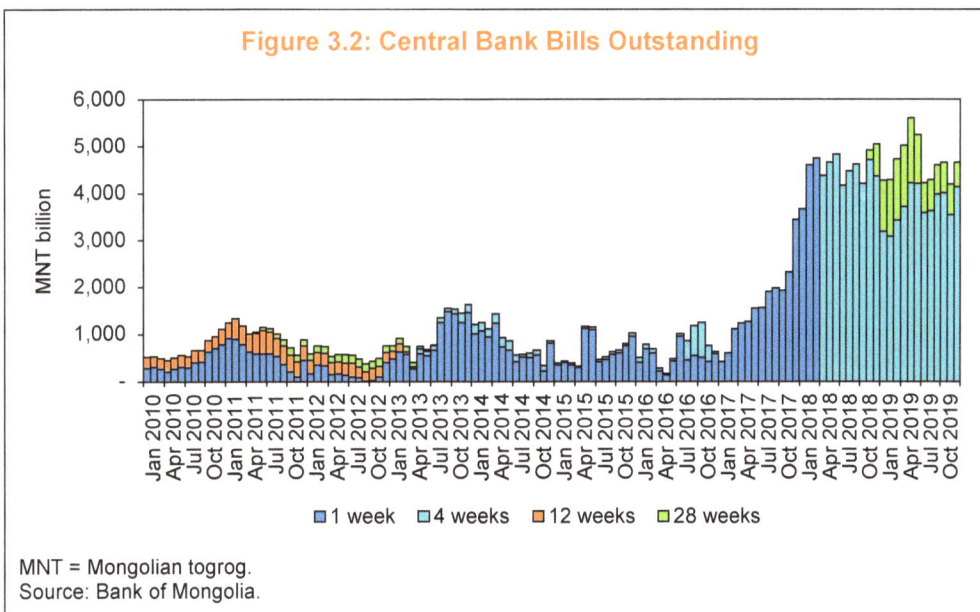

Figure 3.2: Central Bank Bills Outstanding

MNT = Mongolian togrog.
Source: Bank of Mongolia.

2.   Repurchase Agreements

A repo is a contract to sell and, subsequently, repurchase securities at a predetermined date and price. Repos for government bonds and CBBs are conducted through the BOM trading platform and the transfer of ownership is recorded with the MCSD. The BOM also participates in the interbank repo market.

Repo transactions at the interbank market are standardized by the domestic repurchase master agreement developed by the BOM. Repo transactions have terms up to 1 year in the interbank money market.

The volume of interbank repo transactions for CBBs has picked up since 2017, while government bond repo volumes have dropped since the government temporarily halted new government bond issuance. In 2016, the total volume of CBB repo transactions was MNT1.2 trillion, comprising 13.5% of total interbank transactions. This increased to MNT6.5 trillion, or 24.5% of total interbank transactions, in 2019. There have been no government bond repo transactions on the interbank market since 2018.

3.   Overnight Lending

Banks make overnight lending to each other to cover their short-term reserve shortages. The overnight interest rate is lower than the repo financing rate provided by the BOM and does not require any collateral. Therefore, banks enter into interbank overnight lending agreements to facilitate the efficient use of free resources and meet mandatory reserve requirements.

Interbank overnight lending is regulated by the BOM Regulation on Interbank Overnight Lending. Transactions and settlement are conducted via the BOM trading platform.

Overnight lending was the primary method for banks to transact in the interbank market prior to 2018, constituting 60.0% of total interbank transaction volume in 2016 and 51.4% in 2017. However, due to the increase in CBB issuance and CBB repo transactions, overnight lending transactions accounted for only 18.2% of total interbank transaction volume in 2019. There was a total of MNT4.9 trillion in overnight lending in the interbank market in 2019.

4.   Interbank Deposits

Interbank collateralized deposits are made between banks for the purposes of collateral. These transactions are similar to repo transactions, but instead of selling the underlying securities with repos, banks deposit the securities for collateral purposes as part of a collateralized interbank loan. Collateral for interbank deposits are typically CBBs, in which case the BOM registers and locks the collateral assets based on the contract between the banks. Interbank uncollateralized deposits are made in a similar manner as overnight lending between banks, but with longer maturities.

In 2019, the total transaction volume of interbank deposits at the interbank market was MNT1.6 trillion, comprising 5.9% of total interbank transaction volume, up from MNT0.8 trillion and 9.3% in 2016.

D.   Segmentation of the Market

The Mongolian bond market can be divided into government bonds, CBBs, publicly offered corporate debt instruments, and privately placed corporate debt instruments. At the time of writing, there were no publicly offered corporate debt securities in the domestic bond market. Although privately placed corporate debt instruments are common, there are no official data available as these instruments are not regulated. Table 3.1 provides an overview of the market by types of debt instrument.

Table 3.1: Outstanding Value of Debt Instruments in Mongolia
(MNT billion)

	Outstanding Value (MNT billion)
Government bonds	1,435.0
Central bank bills	4,663.5
Publicly offered corporate debt securities	–
Privately placed corporate debt instruments (Privately placed corporate debt securities registered with the MCSD)	Not available
(Privately placed corporate debt instruments, other than corporate debt securities, not registered with the MCSD)	(Not officially available)[a]

MCSD = Mongolian Central Securities Depository, MNT = Mongolian togrog.
[a] According to the Financial Regulatory Commission, the total outstanding amount of privately placed debt instruments issued by non-banking financial institutions was MNT23.5 billion at the end of December 2018.
Note: All data as of the end of December 2019.
Sources: Government of Mongolia; Ministry of Finance; Bank of Mongolia; Mongolian Stock Exchange; and Mongol Securities Exchange.

E.   Methods of Issuing Debt Instruments (Primary Market)

Government bonds in Mongolia are issued by auction method, predefined rate (noncompetitive method), and private placement.

Corporate debt instruments, both public offerings and private placements, are mainly offered through underwriters at a predefined rate.

1.   Government Bonds

Prior to the temporary cessation of government bond issuance in 2017, the MOF issued government bonds as per the Regulation on Issuance and Trading of Government Securities (approved 26 November 2014, repealed and replaced on 20 February 2019), which was approved under the Joint Decree of the Minister of Finance and Governor of the Bank of Mongolia. Under this regulation, government bonds were issued through exchange and off-exchange methods. Off-exchange issuance was conducted through the interbank OTC market of the BOM, while exchange issuance was conducted through the MSE. Registration and transfer of ownership were made at the MCSD, and the BOM handled the cash settlement process.

Government bond issuance schedules for the next 6 months are announced by the MOF through its website,[24] the MSE website,[25] the BOM website,[26] and other media outlets on 31 January and 30 June of each year.

With the Regulation on Primary and Secondary Market Operations of Domestic Government Securities (approved 20 February 2019), there is no longer a distinction between exchange and off-exchange issuance of government bonds. The new regulation does not specify whether government bonds are to be auctioned through the MSE or the BOM. The MOF is free to choose the issuing venue for the public issuance and auction of government bonds. Private placements of short-term government bonds are issued directly to the BOM or with the approval of the

---

[24] Government of Mongolia, MOF. Securities. https://mof.gov.mn/article/securities/unet-tsaas-huvaari.
[25] Government of Mongolia, MSE. http://www.mse.mn/mn/content/list/227.
[26] BOM. https://www.mongolbank.mn/governmentbond.aspx.

government. However, the new regulation has yet to be applied in practice and will commence when government bond issuance restarts.

a.   Central Bank of Mongolia

Prior to the temporary issuance halt in 2017, off-exchange issuances of government bonds were conducted on a weekly basis through the BOM interbank OTC market by auction method. Banks were direct participants in the OTC market, and banks could take orders from other investors as indirect participants. Government bond primary auctions used to take place every Wednesday (as per the schedule released by the MOF).

Under the newly approved Regulation on Primary and Secondary Market Operations of Domestic Government Securities, the MOF will choose the issuing venue for public issuance and auction of government bonds. The private placement of short-term government bonds will be issued directly to the BOM.

b.   Mongolian Stock Exchange

Prior to the temporary issuance halt in 2017, exchange issuances of government bonds were conducted through the MSE. The MOF could choose the issuance method of government bonds on the MSE, either auction or noncompetitive bidding. Typically, issuance through the exchange was done by noncompetitive bidding, where the auction results of the off-exchange issuance were used to determine the interest rates for the exchange issuance. There have been only three instances of government bonds being offered by competitive bidding method on the MSE, all of which were in 2017 shortly before the MOF temporarily halted LCY government bond issuance under the IMF bailout program.

Based on the issuers' (MOF) request to list government securities, the CEO of the MSE resolves to list and issue government bonds in the primary market. This resolution is then sent to the MCSD to register the government bonds. After the primary market issuance sessions, the MSE sends the order blotter to the MOF, which allocates the orders. Investors participated in the primary market issuance of the exchange-traded government bonds through MSE member securities firms.

Under the previous Regulation on Issuance and Trading of Government Securities, the exchange issuance of government bonds was conducted through the MSE from 2015 to 2017. It is expected that government bond primary market issuance will continue to go through the MSE once the issuance restarts, although the new regulation is yet to be applied in practice.

c.   Private Placement of Government Bonds

Private placement of government bonds is possible under the current Government Regulation on Primary and Secondary Market Operations of Domestic Government Securities. The MOF can issue government bonds by private placement to the BOM and the Social Security Fund of Mongolia, or with approval from the government, as per Article 8 of the regulation.

2.   Corporate Debt Instruments

Corporate debt instruments are required to be approved and registered by the FRC and listed on an exchange to be publicly offered. As per Article 4.1.21 of the Securities Market Law, a public offer (referred to as open) is defined as follows:

"Public offer" means the making of an offer to the public through any media channels for the sale of securities to 50 or more persons through an institution undertaking securities trading in accordance with the procedures issued by the Financial Regulatory Commission.

Private placement (referred to as closed) is regarded as private if the number of investors purchasing the securities is less than 50 and the issuance is not promoted through media outlets. In addition, privately placed debt instruments are not within the scope of the Securities Market Law and therefore follow the Company Law. Typically, privately placed corporate debt instruments do not constitute securities, as they are generally issued based on purchase agreements between the issuer, underwriter, and investors. However, if the privately placed corporate debt instruments are registered at a regulated securities depository entity (MCSD or custodian), it would be considered a security.

Currently, there is no regulated OTC market for corporate debt instruments; however, there is an unregulated OTC market for privately placed corporate debt instruments.

a.   Public Offering

Corporates can issue corporate debt securities by public offer as per Article 16 of the Securities Market Law. The Securities Market Law does not require underwriters for debt securities issuances, unlike equities. In other words, corporates are allowed to register and list their debt securities by themselves, without underwriters. However, due to the lack of expertise, knowledge, and client base, corporates typically appoint underwriters when issuing debt securities publicly.

Underwriters submit all documents required by the FRC Regulation on Securities Registration and the exchange's Listing Rules. Publicly offered corporate debt securities are registered at the MCSD and traded through the exchange.

The FRC does not impose eligibility criteria as it approves securities issuances and listings based on the exchange's opinion to list. Therefore, eligibility criteria are set by the exchange. The criteria to list debt securities on the exchange are explained in detail in Section J of this chapter.

b.   Private Placement

Under current regulations, privately placed corporate debt instruments are not considered to be securities, unless registered at a regulated securities depository entity.

Typically, the private placement of corporate debt instruments is conducted via underwriters or directly to the investors in the form of corporate debt instrument purchase agreements. Most of these agreements are not registered at the MCSD or with a custodian.

Most of these privately placed corporate debt instruments are not legally considered to be securities. Instead, they are negotiable loan agreements legally, as the issuer (borrower), investor (lender), and underwriter all need to agree on every transaction. However, they are referred and marketed as corporate bonds in the Mongolian market.

Because these privately placed corporate debt instruments are not regulated, there are no official data to gauge the development of this market. However, one source of data would be the FRC statistics on NBFIs, which are regulated by the FRC and are one of the primary issuers of privately placed corporate debt instruments. According to the Consolidated Financial Statements for Non-Banking Financial Institutions for the

Year 2018, which is published by the FRC, the total amount of the privately placed debt instruments of NBFIs was MNT23.5 billion in 2018, an increase of 241.4% from the previous year.

F.   Governing Law and Jurisdiction (Debt Instrument Issuance)

1.   Government Bonds

Government bonds are regulated under the Debt Management Law (enacted 18 February 2015). As per Article 26 of the Debt Management Law, the MOF is responsible for formulating regulations for the primary and secondary markets for government securities. The Securities Market Law was amended in 18 February 2015 to remove government and municipal bonds from the list of securities regulated by the law.

2.   Corporate Debt Instruments Issuances by Residents in Mongolia

Public offers of corporate debt instruments are regulated by the FRC, as per the Securities Market Law and the Company Law. Privately placed corporate debt instruments are outside the scope of the Securities Market Law and therefore follow the Company Law (in cases when issuers are Mongolian resident companies).

Therefore, the governing law for resident-issued domestic corporate debt securities is Mongolian law.

3.   Debt Securities Issuances by Nonresidents in Mongolia

Under the Securities Market Law and FRC regulations, foreign-exchange-listed nonresident issuers that are regulated by the International Organization of Securities Commissions member regulator are allowed to issue securities in the Mongolian market with the approval of the FRC.

In such cases, it is not considered that the company is conducting business within Mongolian territory, according to the law. However, there is no specific clause on whether an entity registered but not listed in a foreign jurisdiction is allowed to publicly offer its securities in the Mongolian market; there has been no such case to date.

To regulate and fast-track the process of allowing foreign-exchange-listed nonresident issuers to issue securities in Mongolia, the FRC has approved the Temporary Regulation on Registering Securities Offered in Mongolia by a Foreign Exchange Listed Entity and Securities Offered in a Foreign Country by a Mongolian Exchange Listed Entity on 24 November 2017. However, this regulation is primarily for equity issuances. Article 9.3 of the MSE Listing Rules states that the rules are not applicable to the debt securities of a foreign-listed issuer, debt securities denominated in a foreign currency, and debt securities previously issued on a foreign (nonresident) exchange.

With regard to the domestic bond issuances of nonresident issuers, the governing law regarding the transfer and settlement of securities will be Mongolian law.

G.   Language of Documentation and Disclosure Items

Under current regulations, issuers publicly offering their securities in Mongolia are required to submit the issuance application, documentation, and disclosure items in the Mongolian language.

As private placements are outside the scope of the Securities Market Law, issuers and/or underwriters can choose the documentation language depending on the target investors.

In the case of dual listing for a foreign-exchange-listed nonresident issuer, disclosure information is allowed to be in English, although the main body of the documents are required to be translated into Mongolian.

H.   Accounting Regime Applicable to Corporations in Mongolia

According to the Law on Accounting, business entities and organizations in Mongolia shall adhere to the International Financial Reporting Standards (IFRS). However, small and medium-sized enterprises can follow the International Financial Reporting Standard for Small and Medium-sized Entities, as per the law.

The detailed reporting standards and methodology follow the Guidance of General Accounting Forms and Methodology for Business Entities, revised by the Ministerial Order No. 100, dated 8 May 2018.

Under these regulations, business entities and organizations operating in the territory of Mongolia are required to keep their accounting records in the Mongolian language. Business entities, organizations, and representative offices may record their operations and transactions in foreign currency with the permission of the MOF, according to the Law on Accounting.

I.   Registration of Debt Instruments

This section deals with the concept of registration of securities in the Mongolian bond market, as well as various regulatory requirements to register the debt instruments to ensure recognition of ownership and the ability to trade and settle the debt instruments.

1.   Public Offering Registration with the Financial Regulatory Commission

Under the Securities Market Law and the Regulation on Securities Registration of the FRC, the public offer of corporate debt securities are required to be registered with the FRC, the exchange, and the central depository (MCSD). In the Mongolian context, the term "registration" means both registration and listing.

The issuer is required to get approval from both the FRC and the exchange to publicly offer its securities. Once the FRC approves the issuer to publicly offer its securities, the FRC registers the securities in the register of securities approved for public offer and sends the approval to list the securities to the exchange, as well as to the MCSD to register the securities, according to the Securities Market Law.

The issuer also needs an approval from the exchange to list its securities on the exchange under the current regulations. The issuer is not required to receive a separate approval from the MCSD to register its securities approved by the FRC for public offer, although the issuer needs to send a formal request to the MCSD to register its securities. Chapter II has more details.

2.   Private Placement Registration

Private placements are not required to be registered at any regulatory body under the current regulations. However, to ensure recognition of ownership, some issuers choose to register and deposit their debt instruments at a custodian bank or the MCSD.

As the Securities Market Law regulates and defines securities in general, and privately placed corporate debt instruments are generally issued in practice with a purchase agreement between the issuer, underwriter, and investors, these privately placed debt instruments are not to be deemed as securities under the current regulations.

However, if the privately placed corporate debt instruments are registered at an FRC-regulated securities depository entity, then the debt instruments can be deemed as securities under the Securities Market Law. As per the law, registration at a depository entity is legal proof of ownership of the securities.

3.   Securities Registration with Securities Depository

According to Article 45.9 of the Securities Market Law, publicly offered securities are required to be registered with the central depository (MCSD). This means that securities, including publicly offered debt instruments, will need to be registered with the MCSD upon getting the approval of the FRC. Privately placed debt instruments are not legally required to be registered at the central depository (MCSD), although registering at the central depository would be legal proof of ownership of the securities.

J.   Listing of Debt Instruments

Government bonds are listed on the MSE, which was selected by the MOF as the venue for exchange issuance of its bonds under the 2014 Government Regulation on Issuance and Trading of Government Securities. The MOF started issuing government bonds through the MSE in 2015 to support the LCY bond market until the temporary halt of government securities issuance under the IMF's EFF in October 2017.

As of December 2019, there were 11 LCY government bonds worth a total of MNT34.2 billion, with maturities of 3 and 5 years, listed on the MSE. Weighted-average interest rates for the government bonds listed on the MSE were 15.5% for 3-year bonds and 16.8% for 5-year bonds.

All publicly offered corporate debt securities are listed on the exchange as required by the Securities Market Law. Publicly offered debt securities can be listed on either the government-owned MSE or the new, privately owned MSX, which started operations in 2015. As of December 2019, there were no publicly offered corporate debt securities listed on either exchange.

The listing of publicly offered corporate debt securities on the MSE started in 2001. There have been 15 publicly offered corporate debt securities totaling MNT24.6 billion listed in its history (Table 3.2). These listed corporate debt securities were issued with small denominations (face value), as almost all corporate debt securities issuances were targeted to retail investors.

For the MSX, there has been only one publicly offered corporate debt securities listing, as the private exchange is a relatively new entrant to the market.

Table 3.2: Corporate Debt Securities Listing History at the Mongolian Stock Exchange

No.	Issuer Name	Maturity (months)	Interest Rate (%)	Face Value[a]	Total Amount (MNT)	Interest Payment	Issue Year
1	Barilga Corporation JSC	10	19.6	MNT10,000	5,335,680,000	At maturity	2001
2	Niislel Urguu JSC	12	19.7	MNT5,000	1,200,000,000	Semiannual	2002
7	Altan Khot Corporation LLC	8	19.8	MNT10,000	996,920,000	At maturity	2002
9	Ikh Barilga Tusul LLC	8	19.8	MNT50,000	1,300,000,000	At maturity	2003
3	Puma Group LLC	12	21.6	MNT10,000	1,000,000,000	Quarterly	2004
4	MCS Electronics LLC	18	19.0	MNT120,000	872,640,000	Semiannual	2004
5	MCS Electronics LLC	12	11.0	USD100	605,000,000	At maturity	2004
6	Anod Bank	24	19.6	MNT10,000	209,490,000	Semiannual	2004
8	Gobi JSC	12	19.2	MNT10,000	1,000,000,000	Semiannual	2005
10	Moninjbar JSC	18	21.6	MNT10,000	500,000,000	Quarterly	2005
11	Monfresh Juice LLC	12	11.0	USD10	182,811,800	Semiannual	2007
12	Moninjbar JSC	24	11.2	MNT10,000	502,000,000	Semiannual	2008
13	Just Agro LLC	12	16.2	MNT10,000	4,394,540,000	Quarterly	2011
14	Erchim Engineering LLC	12	18.5	MNT10,000	457,750,000	At maturity	2015
15	Suu JSC	12	17.5	MNT100,000	6,000,000,000	At maturity	2017

JSC = joint stock company, LLC = limited liability company, MNT = Mongolian togrog, USD = United States dollar.
[a] Face value refers to the minimum denomination.
Source: Mongolian Stock Exchange.

1.   Conditions for Debt Instruments Listing

The requirements for corporate debt securities listing are regulated by the Securities Market Law, FRC Regulation on Securities Registration, and Securities Listing Rules of the exchange.

According to Article 16 of the Securities Market Law, the following requirements must be met to offer corporate debt instruments by public offer:

(i)   A company that has met the criteria determined by the FRC and the exchange may issue debt instruments for public offer.

(ii)   The total value of debt instruments being issued by a company for public offer shall not be greater than the relevant company's net asset value. The total value of debt instruments for public offer being issued with a third-party guarantee shall not be greater than the total sum of the amount of the relevant company's net asset value and the total guarantees issued by the third party.

The FRC shall issue permission to issue and then trade the securities on the securities market, and such permission shall be granted on the basis of a request from the securities issuer and subsequent confirmation to the FRC from the exchange at which the securities are registered in the stock exchange registration system and the relevant preparations are finalized, as per the law. This process constitutes the securities listing and trading permission of the FRC.

Detailed requirements on the contents of the securities prospectus can be found in Chapter II.F. Furthermore, the application to register securities for public offer needs to meet the requirements set by the FRC and the exchange in accordance with the respective rules and regulations.

As per Article 14 of the MSE Listing Rules, debt securities and the issuer shall meet the following criteria:

(i) The issuer of debt securities shall meet the same requirements as the Board II equity listing, as follows:
  (a) The issuer shall have stable operations in its industry for a minimum of 2 years prior to the date of listing application.
  (b) The financial reports for the most recent 2 financial years shall be prepared in accordance with the IFRS and verified by an auditing firm along with an audit report. In the case of a foreign-listed issuer being listed on an exchange approved by the FRC, the financial reports are accepted if prepared in accordance with a different accounting standard that is accepted by the foreign (nonresident) exchange. In such a case, the issuer shall report material changes in the financial report that are caused by any difference between the IFRS and the accounting standards under which the reports were originally prepared.
  (c) The issuer shall have sufficient working capital for running its business operations for at least 12 months after the listing or must have a net profit of no less than MNT100 million.
  (d) The issuer shall comply with Mongolian corporate governance principles or explain if it is not in compliance.
  (e) Mining companies shall also meet the following criteria in addition to the above:
    i.   minimum of 5 years operational proved or probable reserves as evaluated by an independent specialized expert,
    ii. no less than 30% of the asset structure shall be equity, and
    iii. no less than MNT1.5 billion worth of net tangible assets.

(ii) If the debt securities issuer fails to meet all of the Criteria for Board II equity listing requirements, the issuer must meet one of the following criteria:
  (a) The issuer shall have conducted its main operations for no less than 3 years and hold sufficient collateral assets to guarantee full repayment of the principal and interest payments for the debt securities.
  (b) The issuer shall be fully guaranteed by the Government of Mongolia.
  (c) The debt securities offered to the public shall be insured by more than 80% of its total value.

(iii) The debt securities shall meet following criteria:
  (a) There shall be no restrictions on the free movement and trading of the securities, such as pledge and seal, and the securities shall be freely transferable and tradable.
  (b) The value of the debt securities offered to the public shall meet the conditions set out in Article 16.4 of the Securities Market Law.
  (c) In the case of offering debt securities, an underwriter may not be required depending on the scale of the offering and the nature of the issuer.
  (d) In the case of convertible securities, the shares for future conversion shall be listed on the MSE and meet the requirements and conditions set out in Article 39 of the Company Law.
  (e) The issuer may be required to provide collateral for the property and property rights, or provide an independent third-party guarantee in

case the MSE considers the debt securities would have potential adverse impact on the rights and interests of the investors.

(iv)　The issuer and the regulated person providing professional services to the issuer are entitled to make a request on reasonable grounds for exemptions and waivers from listing criteria for shares and debt securities set in the MSE Listing Rules.

(v)　The listing criteria outlined on Board I and II listing requirements may be waived or exempted when:
   (a)　the issuing company will implement infrastructure projects that are of high significance to national and/or regional economic development,
   (b)　the MSE considers the issuer to be of high interest to the investors and there is a strong demand in the market for the securities of the issuer,
   (c)　there is a secondary listing by a foreign-listed issuer, and
   (d)　the company's operations support the implementation of the United Nations Sustainable Development Goals.

According to the MSX Listing Rules (approved 24 May 2018), the following requirements must be met to issue debt instruments, as per Article 16:

(i)　The issuer—in the case of issuance of secured debt instruments, the issuer and the guarantor—shall be properly established and registered in accordance with the procedures established by the relevant legislation of the country of origin.

(ii)　If the issuer—in the case of issuance of secured debt instruments, the issuer and the guarantor—is not listed on the MSE, their business is required to be considered suitable by the MSE.

(iii)　The issuer has been operating for at least 3 fiscal years.

(iv)　The issuer—in the case of issuance of secured debt instruments, the issuer and the guarantor—shall submit to the MSE audited financial statements for the last 3 years. In special cases, the MSE may accept 2-year financial statements.

(v)　New applicants must submit registration documents to the MSE within 6 months of the submission of last financial year's financial statements.

(vi)　The equity capital of the issuer—in the case of issuance of secured debt instruments, the equity capital of the guarantor—shall not be less than MNT1 billion and the nominal value of the debt instrument shall not be less than MNT500 million. This requirement does not apply if additional debt instruments are being issued.

(vii)　A person purchasing a debt instrument shall have the right to freely dispose of the debt instrument.

(viii)　The issuer may issue debt instruments with conditions of conversion into shares.

(ix)　If the issuer issues a convertible debt instrument, it must fully comply with the requirements set forth in Article 39 of the Company Law.

The detailed requirements for the application form and application documents are set out in Section 7 of the MSX Listing Rules.

2.　Procedure for Debt Instruments Listing Registration

This section details the individual steps necessary to list publicly offered debt securities on the exchanges in Mongolia, as outlined in the Securities Market Law, FRC Regulation on Securities Registration, and the Securities Listing Rules of the exchange.

Step 1—Submission of Application to the Financial Regulatory Commission and the Exchange

a.   Application to the Financial Regulatory Commission

The following documents shall be appended to an application to register securities in the register of securities approved for public offer, according to the Securities Market Law (amended 24 May 2013):

(i)   application form,
(ii)   securities prospectus,
(iii)   document evidencing payment of the regulatory service fee, and
(iv)   other documents as specified in regulations issued by the FRC.

According to the FRC Regulation on Securities Registration (amended 23 November 2015, effective 1 January 2016), the following documents are required to be appended to an application to register securities for public offer:

(i)   application form for securities registration (Form FRC03101);
(ii)   securities prospectus prepared in accordance with the requirements set by the exchange;
(iii)   shareholders' decision to issue securities, or make changes to its securities, along with related evidence;
(iv)   legal opinion required by Article 4.2.2 of the regulation;
(v)   business and asset valuation report, and audit report prepared in accordance with the requirements set by the exchange;
(vi)   report of a third-party analyst or professional, if the third-party analyst or professional has conducted a research report in accordance with Article 10.8 of the Securities Market Law; and
(vii)   document evidencing payment of the regulatory service fee.

Moreover, the FRC requires the issuer to submit all contracts and agreements between the issuer and third-party advisors (underwriter, audit firm, legal firm, and valuation firm) to review whether the contracts have been signed in accordance with the relevant laws and whether the roles and responsibilities of each party have been properly defined.

b.   Application to the Mongolian Stock Exchange

The issuer must apply and get approval from the exchange for the listing of its debt securities. The listing process is regulated by the MSE Listing Rules. According to Article 3.2 of the MSE Listing Rules (approved 25 January 2018), the following documents are required to be appended to an application to list securities for public offer:

(i)   application form for securities listing (Form 2);
(ii)   issuer's declaration (Form 3);
(iii)   underwriter's declaration (Form 4);
(iv)   listing decision by the issuer's competent authority;
(v)   securities prospectus;
(vi)   legal opinion as specified in Article 2.6 of the MSE Listing Rules;
(vii)   valuation report as specified in Article 2.7 of the MSE Listing Rules;
(viii) conclusions and opinions as specified in Article 2.4 of the MSE Listing Rules, where applicable; and
(ix)   document evidencing payment of the listing application fee as specified in Article 22.2.1 of the MSE Listing Rules.

The documents specified above may not be provided if the securities are issued or fully guaranteed by the Government of Mongolia.

The application for listing and the securities prospectus shall be signed and sealed by the issuers' chair of the board of directors, CEO, chief financial officer (or chief accountant), and the CEO of the underwriter (if any).

Detailed requirements on the contents of securities prospectus can be found in Chapter II.F.

c. Application to the Mongol Securities Exchange

According to the MSX Listing Rules (approved 24 May 2018), the following documents are required to be submitted to the MSX for the review of the application for listing:

(i)   two copies of the draft registration document with the complete inclusion of the relevant information specified in Chapter XVIII and Appendix 6-A of the MSX Listing Rules;

(ii)   two copies of the draft official notice;

(iii) two copies of the draft debt instrument purchase order sheet;

(iv)   two copies of documents and guarantees prepared in accordance with Appendix 4 of the MSX Listing Rules;

(v)   two copies of the statement of adjustment by a certified accountant if an adjustment has been made to the certified accountant's opinion;

(vi)   certified copy of financial statements, correction statements, real estate valuation report, contract, and official decision;

(vii) proof of commitment signed by each member of the issuer's board and each authorized person regarding their biography;

(viii) debt instrument guarantee and other related documents;

(ix)   certified copy of state registration certificate or its equivalent;

(x)   certified copy of an operating permit;

(xi)   certified copy of the company's charter, memorandum, and similar documents; and

(xii) an application form made in accordance with Form 3-3.

The detailed requirements for the application form and application documents are set out in Article 7 of the MSX Listing Rules.

Step 2—Review of Application and Approval by the Financial Regulatory Commission and the Exchange

The FRC shall review and issue a decision within 20 working days of receipt of the required documents and the securities prospectus, according to Article 9.6 of the Securities Market Law. When a decision refusing to register the securities has been made by the FRC, it must specify justifiable grounds for the decision. The period for considering applications shall be calculated as commencing on the date of receipt of a complete application.

However, the period for considering applications may be extended by up to a maximum of 15 working days by the FRC, if the FRC deems it necessary to obtain additional documents, valuations, or other reports from the issuer or independent experts and advisors as per the law.

Based on the FRC's decision to register the securities, the actual securities registration is made at the FRC, the exchange, and the central depository. The securities trading code is issued by the exchange, while the International Securities Identification Number is issued by the MCSD. When the securities issuance is approved by the FRC for public offer, the decision is delivered to the issuer, the exchange, and the MCSD, and the decision is made public through the FRC website.

The exchange shall review and issue a decision whether to accept or refuse the securities listing application within 14 working days, according to Article 3.2.3 of the FRC Regulation on Securities Registration. The start date of the review shall be the day of the submission of complete documents that meet the relevant requirements. If necessary, the exchange may conduct an onsite inspection and request clarifications and additional documentation from the company management in relation to the securities and the use of proceeds from the offering and may obtain evidence in a form of a meeting or an interview. If an exchange's decision to accept the listing has been made, it must deliver the decision along with its opinion to the FRC within 2 working days.

The review period may be extended by 15 business days in case of a request for additional documentation, independent expert opinions, and reports such as an audit report and valuation report that are necessary for making a listing decision.

Step 3—Actual (Effective) Listing

The FRC shall approve the commencement of primary market issuance within 2 business days, based on the (i) official notification by the exchange of the listing of the securities and completion of necessary preparations for the commencement of trading as per Article 12.2 of the Securities Market Law, and (ii) the issuer's official request to commence the trading of the securities to the FRC.

The exchange shall sign the listing agreement with the issuer to list the securities and deliver the copy of the listing decision to the MCSD. The securities shall be assigned a name and a symbol, taking into account the issuer's request. Debt securities shall be listed by the name of the instrument and the name shall contain the maturity, coupon rate, and coupon payment frequency.

After the primary market issuance is completed, the underwriter is required to submit a trading report to the FRC within 3 working days, as outlined in the FRC Regulation on Securities Registration. Secondary market trading cannot commence until the FRC approves the primary market issuance as successful.

If the FRC deems that the primary market issuance does not meet the requirements set in the FRC Regulation on Securities Registration and the relevant laws, it can invalidate and cancel the primary market issuance. The FRC deems the primary market offer successful if all funds necessary to be raised by the public offer have been transferred to the respective account of the issuer, as per the Securities Market Law. Once the offer is deemed successful by the FRC, secondary market trading can commence.

Due to these steps required by the FRC Regulation on Securities Registration, there is typically a gap of a few days between the primary market issuance and secondary market trading of the publicly offered securities.

3.   Listing of Government Bonds

Exchange-traded government bonds are listed on the MSE. As per Article 9.2 of the Listing Rules of MSE, debt securities issued or fully guaranteed by the government shall be listed and traded on the MSE per approval from the MOF. Based on the issuers' (MOF) request to list government securities, the CEO of the MSE resolves to list and issue government bonds in the primary market. As government securities are not regulated by the Securities Market Law, the usual requirements for listing of securities, such as a securities prospectus, are not required for government bonds. Guidelines on Primary Market Issuance of Government Securities of the MSE details the trading types, participants, and settlement of government bonds at the MSE.

K. Methods of Trading Debt Instruments (Secondary Market)

Secondary market trading of government bonds occurs in the BOM interbank OTC market for off-exchange issuances and through the MSE for exchange issuances. Exchange trades follow the secondary market trading rules of the MSE.

For publicly offered corporate debt securities, the process follows the secondary market trading rules of the respective exchanges, either the MSE or MSX.

There is no dedicated marketplace for secondary market trading of privately placed corporate debt instruments, as these are legally not securities and are typically not registered at the central depository of securities. Typically, holders of these privately placed corporate debt instruments sign a tri-party purchase agreement including the issuer and the underwriter to purchase, and another purchase agreement to sell the debt instruments before maturity. Since privately placed corporate debt instruments are typically issued with a maturity of 3–18 months, most investors tend to hold these debt instruments to maturity.

1. Trading on the Exchanges

Government bonds issued by the exchange are listed and traded on the MSE, under the previous 2014 Government Regulation on Issuance and Trading of Government Securities. However, with the new 2019 Government Regulation on Primary and Secondary Market Operations of Domestic Government Securities, the issuer (MOF) chooses the organizer of government securities trading and removed the distinction between exchange issuance and off-exchange issuance. If the MOF chooses the MSE as the organizer of government securities trading when government securities issuance restarts, then the trading will go through the MSE.

The trading of listed government and corporate debt securities on the exchanges is carried out by the trading members of the exchanges, both retail and institutional investors, and are governed by the respective trading rules of the exchanges.

2. Over-the-Counter Market

Secondary market trading of off-exchange issuance of government bonds was regulated by the Regulation on Secondary Market Trading of Government Securities, approved by Joint Decree of the Minister of Finance, Governor of the Central Bank, and Chair of the Financial Regulatory Committee on 21 May 2013. The off-exchange trading of government bonds previously took place among commercial banks on the BOM interbank OTC market.

However, with the new 2019 Government Regulation on Primary and Secondary Market Operations of Domestic Government Securities, primary market issuance and secondary market trading of government securities are now regulated by this single regulation. If the MOF chooses the BOM as the organizer of government securities trading when government securities issuance restarts, then trading will take place in the interbank OTC market.

The BOM interbank OTC market is only accessible by commercial banks, and there is no OTC marketplace for corporate debt instruments. Market participants such as the MSE and the MASD are currently in the process of developing regulations to introduce an OTC marketplace in the Mongolian capital market.

L.   Debt Instruments Pricing

Mongolia does not have a dedicated bond or securities pricing agency and related regulations. Government bond pricing at issuance is decided by the market participants via auction method, while corporate debt instruments are typically issued by noncompetitive bidding method.

Pricing information of debt securities in Mongolia can be found at their respective trading platforms, while LCY government bond yield curve information can be found on the Bloomberg terminal. The BOM and MOF have officially published LCY government bond yield curve information on the Bloomberg terminal since September 2015, accessible through the CRVF function and then selecting "MNT Mongolian Govt. Bond BVAL Yield Curve" under Mongolia, or by entering the code "GC BI1204."

M.   Transfers of Interest in Debt Instruments

1.   Listed Debt Instruments

Under the Securities Market Law, publicly offered securities are required to be registered at the central depository for securities. This means that securities, including publicly offered debt instruments, will need to be registered by the issuer with the MCSD upon issuance. In addition, government bonds are also registered at the MCSD.

Transfer of ownership of government bonds and publicly listed corporate debt instruments can take place through both trading and nontrading methods.

In the case of trading, both exchange trades and BOM interbank OTC trades were previously prefunded and settled at T+1, and ownership transferred by the MCSD.

The nontrading method includes gifting and inheriting securities regulated under the FRC Regulation on Gifting and Inheriting of Ownership Rights and MCSD Regulation on Registration of Ownership Rights.

2.   Private Placements

As the Securities Market Law regulates and defines securities in general, and privately placed corporate debt instruments are generally issued in practice with a purchasing agreement between the issuer, underwriter, and investors, these privately placed debt instruments are not deemed to be securities under current regulations.

Typically, holders of these privately placed corporate debt instruments sign a tri-party purchase agreement including the issuer and the underwriter to purchase, and another purchase agreement to sell the debt instruments before its maturity. Registration of ownership is performed by either the issuer or the underwriter, and proof of ownership is ensured by the purchase agreement.

However, if the privately placed corporate debt instruments are registered at a regulated securities depository entity (MCSD or custodian) that is regulated by the FRC, then the debt instruments can be deemed to be securities under the Securities

Market Law. As per the law, registration at a depository entity is legal proof of ownership of the securities. In this case, custodians ensure the transfer of ownership upon receiving the purchase agreements.

Private placements are not required to be registered at any regulatory body under the current regulations. However, to ensure recognition of ownership, some issuers choose to register and deposit their debt instruments at a custodian bank or the MCSD.

N.   Market Participants

1.   Issuers

Mongolian bond market issuers are the government and corporates. Government bonds are issued by the MOF under the Debt Management Law. As per the 7 September 2016 amendment to the Debt Management Law, provinces and the capital city are not allowed to issue debt securities. Corporate debt instruments can be either publicly offered or privately placed under the Securities Market Law.

a.   Government

Government bonds (referred to as government securities) are issued by the MOF (referred to as the issuer) in accordance with the Debt Management Law and for the purposes of financing budget deficits, financing seasonal shortfalls in budget revenues, supporting the domestic government securities market, debt refinancing, financing national investment programs, increasing the net foreign currency reserves of the BOM for the purpose of supporting the national balance of payments, and recapitalizing banks by the state in accordance with the Banking Sector Stability Law.

According to the Debt Management Law, the total amount of government bonds to be issued for the year is required to be included in the state budget prepared by the MOF and approved by the Parliament in accordance with the debt ceiling for each fiscal year. The issuance schedule is approved by the MOF, and the bonds are issued in a periodic manner.

The MOF is both the issuer of and the regulator for government bonds in the Mongolian capital market. As of December 2019, there were a total of MNT1.4 trillion worth of LCY government bonds outstanding.

b.   Corporate

Corporate debt instruments are issued by joint stock companies, limited liability companies, and state-owned enterprises under the Securities Market Law and the Company Law. Corporate debt instruments can be publicly offered (referred to as open) or privately placed (referred to as closed).

Issuers of publicly offered corporate debt instruments are regulated by the FRC under the Securities Market Law. Since the current regulations do not differentiate between issuers of publicly offered corporate debt instruments and a publicly listed company, issuers of publicly offered corporate debt instruments are required to meet the same requirements as a listed company. As such, corporate issuers tend to prefer private placement of debt instruments over public offering.

As of December 2019, there are no publicly offered corporate debt instruments outstanding at the exchanges, while there has been a total of 16 publicly offered corporate debt instrument issuances at the MSE and the MSX throughout the history of the Mongolian capital market.

2.   Investors

The bond investor profile in Mongolia depends largely on the type of bond. For government bonds, the largest investors are commercial banks. For corporate debt instruments, the largest investors are local individual investors. Although foreign investors have been more active in recent years, most of their investment is focused on the more secure government bonds.

a.   Banks

Commercial banks are the largest investors in the government bond market in Mongolia. Banks can participate in the government bond market either through the BOM interbank OTC market or the MSE. The off-exchange issuance of government bonds through the BOM interbank OTC market is only accessible to commercial banks. As of December 2019, MNT1.5 trillion of government securities were being held on banks' balance sheets, compared to MNT34.2 billion of government securities outstanding at the MSE.

Banks do not usually invest in corporate debt instruments, as typical corporate debt instruments are treated in the same manner as a regular commercial loan among the banks.

b.   Insurance Companies

Under the FRC Regulation on Requirements for Investments Made by the Insurance Company Reserve Funds (amended 17 July 2013), insurance companies can invest reserve funds in debt instruments with certain limits. As per this regulation, insurance companies are allowed to invest 100% of their reserve funds in government securities, but only up to 20% of their reserve funds in corporate debt instruments (securities).

Market participation in the domestic capital market by insurance companies is low, as these companies prefer to keep their reserve funds in bank deposits due to liquidity constraints in the domestic capital market.

c.   Social Security Fund

There are no regulations currently available that require the Social Security Fund of Mongolia to invest its assets. As such, the excess funds of the Social Security Fund are currently deposited at select commercial banks. It will require a major systemic reform of the social security system to allow the Social Security Fund to invest its assets.

d.   Domestic Individual Investors

As domestic corporate bond market development is in the early stage, and with the lack of professional institutional investors in the market, retail investors are the primary participants in the market for corporate debt instruments, both publicly offered and privately placed. For example, during the last publicly offered corporate debt instrument issuance at the MSE, domestic individual investors were the largest buyers, accounting for 42.5% of the total issuance amount, while domestic banks and corporates comprised 37.1%.

Under the previous Government Regulation on Issuance and Trading of Government Securities, government bonds were issued and traded on the MSE from 2015 to 2017.

When the government bond issuance was temporarily halted in October 2017, domestic individual investors constituted 19.8% of primary market trading and 8.9% of secondary market trading of government bonds, while domestic entities formed 76.0% of primary and 88.3% of secondary market trading.

e.   Foreign Investors

Foreign investors have become more active in the Mongolian capital market in recent years, especially in exchange-listed government bond trading and stock trading.

According to the Securities Market Summary of 2018 published by the FRC, foreign investors accounted for 39.2% of the total trading volume of publicly traded securities, including equities, in 2018, up from 4.1% in the previous year. In addition, foreign investors accounted for 7.2% of the secondary market trading volume of government bonds in 2018, compared to 2.8% in 2017.

3.   Parties Involved in Debt Securities Issuance, Trading, and Settlement

According to the Securities Market Law, participants in the public issuance of securities must be regulated by the FRC.

Licensed securities companies offer a range of securities services including underwriting, brokerage, advisory, and trading. Domestic banks offer services such as cash settlement agents or custodians. In addition, audit firms, valuation firms, and legal firms licensed by the FRC also play an important part in issuing securities to the public.

a.   Securities Companies

Securities companies in Mongolia obtain special licenses from the FRC to conduct brokerage, dealer, underwriting, and investment advisory activities. Moreover, employees of securities companies are required to obtain a License to Conduct Brokerage Activities or License to Conduct Investment Advisory Activities from the MASD. As of 2019, there were a total of 53 securities companies with brokerage, 41 with dealer, 24 with underwriting, and 13 with investment advisory licenses.

Investors purchase government bonds and corporate debt securities listed on the MSE through securities companies. Privately placed corporate debt instrument investors sometimes directly trade with the issuer, without any involvement of securities companies.

b.   Underwriters

According to the Securities Market Law, corporate debt instrument issuance does not require underwriters, unlike equity. However, due to a lack of expertise, knowledge, and client base, corporates typically appoint underwriters when issuing debt instruments for public offer.

As of 2019, 24 securities companies and one commercial bank had underwriting licenses from the FRC.

c.   Audit Firms, Asset Valuation Firms, and Legal Firms

Under the Securities Market Law, a public offering of corporate debt instruments is required to provide a securities prospectus, which needs to include an audited financial report, an asset valuation report, and a legal opinion prepared by third-party advisors—an independent audit firm, asset valuation firm, and legal firm, respectively.[27]

The audit firm, asset valuation firm, and legal firm are all required to be licensed by the FRC and independent from each other. Because these reports take time to prepare, the issuer needs to appoint the third-party advisors early in the public offer preparation stage. A list of service providers with licenses can be found on the FRC website.

d.   Banks

Commercial banks act as clearing agents for secondary market trading of stocks, government bonds, and publicly offered corporate debt securities.

Some commercial banks also conduct underwriting services. As of 2019, one commercial bank had an underwriting license, and three subsidiary securities companies of commercial banks had an underwriting license. As commercial banks are not members of the MSE, they contract with securities companies when trading securities.

e.   Depository Members

The MCSD is the central depository organization in Mongolia. Commercial banks are also allowed to offer custodian services under the licenses granted by the FRC. As of 2019, three commercial banks had custodian licenses.

f.   Settlement Members

The MSCH was reorganized as a separate entity in 2016. Prior to this, MSCH was part of the MCSD. The MSCH settles all trading taking place on the MSE.

O.   Definition of Professional Investors in Mongolia

As per Articles 4.1.18 and 4.1.19 of the Securities Market Law, professional investors and professional investment activities are defined in the following manner:

"Professional investment activity" means investing in a professional and efficient manner by the entities specified in Article 4.1.19 of this law other than NBFIs, underwriters, or dealers utilizing funds raised within an investment policy.

"Professional investor" (the literal translation of the Mongolian version is "entity engaged in professional investment activity") means persons that are considered as entities engaged in professional investment activity by law or the FRC such as investment funds, pension funds, banks or persons licensed to undertake activities related to NBFI activities, insurance, underwriting or dealer activities.

There is, however, no definition of high-net-worth individuals in the current regulations in Mongolia.

---

[27] An asset valuation firm is an entity that provides property valuation and appraisal services under a special license. Typically, these firms provide asset valuation for valuing collateral assets and asset appraisal for insurance purposes. For an asset valuation firm to provide valuation services to participants in the securities market, which is considered a regulated activity by law, it is required to have a license from the FRC. In the context of the securities market, asset valuation firms provide a valuation report on properties and assets on the issuer's balance sheet, as well as a business valuation report of the issuer as an enterprise. These requirements are specific to the Mongolian capital market and to a public offering in general.

P.   Credit Rating Requirements

Current regulations do not require any credit ratings on corporate debt instruments issued in Mongolia, mainly due to the absence of domestic credit rating agencies.

Q.   Financial Guarantee Institution

Mongolia does not have a dedicated financial or credit guarantee institution.

According to the Securities Market Law, companies can issue secured corporate debt instruments that are insured or guaranteed by third party. Typically, insurance companies or related companies play the role of insurer or guarantor of corporate debt instruments in the Mongolian market.

R.   Market Features for Investor Protection

There are several measures to protect investors in accordance with the Securities Market Law and with various related regulations.

1.   Information Disclosure of Listed Companies

Under the Securities Market Law, a listed company is a company registered by the FRC to be publicly listed on the exchange at the "register of securities approved for public offer" of the FRC. The term "registration" means both registration and listing at the exchange in the Mongolian language.

According to Article 20 of the Securities Market Law, listed companies have the following general obligations in terms of information disclosure:

(i)   prepare and submit accurate information and reports that are related to the securities' trade to the FRC and disclose to public, in compliance with relevant methods and forms within the specified period;
(ii)   inform the public and shareholders if project implementation has changed from which it has been stated in the securities' prospectus;
(iii)   submit mid-year and annual year-end financial statements, attested by the auditing firm registered with the FRC, to the MSE and the FRC within the period indicated in Article 13 of the Law on Accounting;
(iv)   disclose to the public information regarding the company's operational and financial situation in accordance with regulations set by the FRC;
(v)   disclose shareholder meeting decisions immediately and submit to the FRC and the MSE relevant information and documents within 3 working days after the meeting was held; and
(vi)   report immediately to the public upon acknowledgment of situations that may affect the price and volume of the securities at a notable level (or materially).

The FRC ensures information disclosure of issuers through its Regulations on Information Transparency of Issuers and Regulations on Remote Supervision. The MSE Listing Rules and Regulations on Supervision require issuers to release relevant information to the public.

To protect investors from insider trading and market manipulation, the FRC enforces market participants and capital market professionals to disclose as insider information holders. The FRC also oversees market manipulation as per its Regulations to Prevent Market Manipulation. If a corporate or an individual is proven to have conducted insider trading and market manipulation, the individual or the legal entity is punished under the Securities Market Law (Articles 81.1 and 81.2), the Violations Law (Article 11.10), and the Criminal Law (Articles 18.8 and 18.9).

2.   Dispute Resolution Measures in the Law

Chapters 7 and 8 of the Securities Market Law includes provisions about dispute resolution for matters related to insider trading, market manipulation, and supervision.

The Bankruptcy Law regulates bankruptcy issues, including disputes arising from an impending bankruptcy or its procedures, applicable to enterprises and cooperatives in Mongolia.

The Civil Law, the Immovable Property Pledge Law, and the Movable and Intangible Property Pledge Law regulate collateral-related issues in the event of a default.

There are no financial alternative dispute resolution agencies in Mongolia yet.[28]

3.   National Development Agency of Mongolia

The National Development Agency (NDA)[29] was established by Parliament Decree No. 12, dated 21 July 2016. The NDA operates as a government regulatory agency to ensure the country's economic stability and develop and implement the integrated socioeconomic and investment policy.

The main operational functions of the NDA are to

(i)   develop the comprehensive development policy of Mongolia;
(ii)   determine the priority sectors of the economy and develop the tendency of the sectors' development;
(iii)   develop a regional development policy;
(iv)   plan and develop the primary strategy on integrated investment and foreign direct investment (FDI) policy, and conduct comprehensive activities to attract and promote FDI in the country; and
(v)   develop a policy on public and private partnership and concession, and organize the implementation of concession projects.

The NDA officially opened Invest in Mongolia, One-Stop Service Center on 25 February 2019. The purpose of the one-stop service center is to provide the following public services, according to the NDA:[30]

(i)   provide information and advisory services on the investment legal framework, investment tax, and nontax incentives;
(ii)   maintain the Systemic Investor Response Mechanism, an e-system for investor grievances related to public services;

---

[28] Financial alternative dispute resolution institutions are usually established and operated in accordance with related laws and self-regulatory rules. A financial alternative dispute resolution engages in an out-of-court dispute resolution procedure for customer complaints against financial services providers and disputes between the two parties, with the aim of resolving financial services-related problems in a fair, neutral, simple, and prompt manner. To successfully engage in dispute resolution in financial services, a financial alternative dispute resolution organization must satisfy eight basic requirements: flexibility, speed, simplicity, expertise and quality assurance, ease of access, comprehensiveness, fairness (including independence and transparency), and confidentiality. Therefore, the organization must be designed and operated to satisfy these requirements.
[29] Government of Mongolia, NDA. http://nda.gov.mn/.
[30] Government of Mongolia, NDA. 2019. Your Guide to Invest in Mongolia. http://nda.gov.mn/backend/f/2019.pdf.

(iii)   provide all advisory and procedural services for registration, verification of legal entity, amendments, reference, description, investor's card, and other services to the legal entity with foreign investment;

(iv)   provide tax information and advice, registration of taxpayers, digital signature, reference, description, tax statement, and tax collection of motor vehicles of foreign-invested companies and investors;

(v)   provide information and advice related to visa, visa issuance, residence permission, temporary visitor's registration, and visa extension; and

(vi)   provide information and advice related to social insurance registration, references, and receipts of statements from foreign-invested companies.

4.   Investor Protection Council of Mongolia

The government established the Investor Protection Council as per ordinance No. 136 of the Prime Minister of Mongolia on 22 December 2016 to facilitate investment-related disputes, provide a favorable legal environment to operate a business, and ensure effective and efficient cooperation between the public and the private sectors.

The council is composed of a chair, 16 members, and a secretary. The main formation of the council's operational structure should be the council's session. Decisions are made by a majority of council members during the session. According to the its official website, the following are the duties of the council:[31]

(i)   preview and make a preparatory prognosis on FDI-related issues that will be discussed during the cabinet session;

(ii)   protect foreign investor rights, and analyze and solve their complaints (aside from the cases inspected under court or arbitrage);

(iii)   improve the investment legal system, expel duplications and ruptures of laws, and present investment-related suggestions made by important associations from the cabinet; and

(iv)   make proposition on an execution of laws and resolutions identified with investment and acquaint it to the cabinet; the council's task ought to be perpetual.

The Investor Protection Council was created to promote FDI in Mongolia, and there have been no cases or complaints related to the capital market in Mongolia.

5.   Corporate Governance Standards

The Corporate Governance Code was adopted in 2007 by the FRC and was revised in 2014. [32] As per Decree No. 69 of the Government of Mongolia, dated 9 March 2011, the National Program to Improve Corporate Governance was approved. As part of this program, the National Council for Corporate Governance was established as per Decree No. 187 of the FRC on 16 November 2011. The council is composed of the MOF, BOM, FRC, MASD, MSE, the Mongolian National Chamber of Commerce and Industry, the Government Agency for Policy Coordination on State Property, the Mongolian Association of Non-Banking Financial Institutions, and the Mongolian Association of Insurance Companies. As part of its mission, the council provides corporate governance trainings for company board members and publishes model company charters and board charters to be adopted by joint stock companies.

The Corporate Governance Code of Mongolia was developed based on recommendations and advice provided by international organizations such as the International Finance Corporation, a member of the World Bank Group, best practices of other countries, special features and current actual conditions of Mongolia, and

---

[31] Government of Mongolia, Investor Protection Council. https://ipc.gov.mn/.

[32] Government of Mongolia. 2011. The Corporate Governance Code. http://governance.mn/laws.

upon consideration of such matters as the impacts of corporate governance structure on the economy and the positive influences of market justice on market participants. This code was developed to be used specifically by publicly traded companies (i.e., joint stock companies) and can also be used by limited liability companies and other legal persons upon making certain adjustments to suit their own special features.

According to Article 20.1.10 of the Securities Market Law, listed companies have a general obligation to comply with corporate governance principles endorsed by the FRC. Moreover, according to Article 75.8 of the Company Law, members and the secretary of the board of directors are required to obtain a Corporate Governance Certificate from the National Council for Corporate Governance.

S.   Bondholders Representative and Bond Trustee

There are no provisions in the Company Law in Mongolia related to the bondholders' meeting and bondholders' representative (or bondholders' agent or a bond trustee-like function).

Therefore, the concepts of bondholders' representative, bondholders' agent, or bond trustee are not available in Mongolia under the current legislation. To introduce the concept in Mongolia, the Company Law needs to be amended; a revised law is currently under discussion among the regulators. It is expected that the concept of bond trustee will be introduced in future revisions to the Company Law.

T.   Bankruptcy and Insolvency Provisions

The Law on Bankruptcy was enacted in Mongolia in 1997 and a total of four amendments were made in 2002, 2010, 2015, and 2019. Mongolia's Law on Bankruptcy defines bankruptcy as a civil matter.

According to the Law on Bankruptcy, Article 5.1, the court shall start a bankruptcy case on the following grounds:[33]

(i)   a party that has the right to demand the fulfillment of obligations has submitted a claim to start a bankruptcy case, and

(ii)   the bankrupt company has notified of its inability to meet the obligations and submitted a request to start a bankruptcy case.

The law states that, within 7 days since determining that the bankrupt company is insolvent, the court shall inform the public through mass media (Article 5.5). The court shall organize the first meeting of creditors within 30 days of the public announcement about considering the bankrupt company as insolvent, according to Article 5.5 of the law.

The meeting of creditors shall propose the court to approve the person who satisfies the requirements specified below as a bankruptcy trustee (Articles 8.2, 11.2, and 11.3 of the law):

(i)   The bankruptcy trustee shall be an individual with higher education in law, finance, and economics who does not have financial and economic personal interests in the bankrupt company's activities, or a legal entity

---

[33] The unofficial translation of the Bankruptcy Law of Mongolia, translated by the Foreign Investment and Foreign Trade Agency of Mongolia can be found at https://www.ilo.org/dyn/natlex/docs/ELECTRONIC/ 49341/61851/F1601145553/MNG49341%20ENG.pdf.

that has the rights and responsibilities to provide professional consulting services in the field of law, finance, and economics.

(ii) The following persons and their family members shall be disqualified from being appointed as a trustee:

(a) bankrupt company's and creditors' management and management members,

(b) members of the bankrupt company that are legal entities other than joint stock companies, and

(c) individual creditors.

The bankruptcy trustee shall have the following rights and responsibilities (Article 12.1 of the law):

(i) take under custody the assets of the bankrupt company according to the court order;

(ii) safeguard the bankrupt company's assets and relevant documents, and conduct counting;

(iii) if required, conduct a documentary audit of the bankrupt company's activities and organize such work;

(iv) announce and convene a meeting of creditors;

(v) approach the court on the issues to be resolved by court;

(vi) review contracts and transactions conducted prior to the start of a bankruptcy case, submit to the meeting of creditors' proposals on whether to terminate, amend, or consider invalid the contracts and transactions specified in Articles 19 and 20 of this law and Articles 43 and 44 of the Civil Code;

(vii) open a special account and deposit the bankrupt company's cash;

(viii) conduct contracts and transactions with others on behalf of the bankrupt company within the scope of the rights granted by the creditors' meeting;

(ix) obtain from the bankrupt company relevant data and documents;

(x) submit to appropriate parties his or her assessment of the bankrupt company;

(xi) evaluate the bankrupt company's assets;

(xii) appoint an assistant within the limits of compensation determined by the creditors;

(xiii) sell the bankrupt company's assets according to the procedures set forth in the Civil Code and Article 18 of this law; and

(xiv) other rights and responsibilities set forth in law.

If it is considered that recapitalization of the bankrupt company and continuing its operations will better meet the requirements of the claim as compared to liquidation, creditors who claim one-third or more of the total payment claimed from the bankrupt company, or bankruptcy trustee, may submit to the court a request for recapitalizing the bankrupt company within 60 days since the date the company was declared bankrupt (Article 23.1 of the Bankruptcy Law).

In such cases, a recapitalization plan must be submitted to the court within 30 days of the date of reviewing the bankruptcy trustee's conclusion. The recapitalization process should be completed within 2 years (Articles 24.1 and 25.1 of the Bankruptcy Law). The court shall decide whether to approve the recapitalization plan within 20 days of its discussion at the meeting of creditors (Article 28.1 of the Bankruptcy Law). The court shall issue an order to consider the recapitalization plan bankrupt and liquidate if it does not approve the recapitalization plan (Article 28.5 of the Bankruptcy Law).

According to Article 32.1 of the Bankruptcy Law, the court shall terminate the recapitalization activities on the following grounds:

(i) implementation of the recapitalization plan has become impossible;

(ii) the recapitalization plan has been implemented completely; and

(iii)   the creditors' claims have been satisfied completely even though the recapitalization plan's implementation is not completed.

In the event of completion of the recapitalization plan, the court shall dismiss the bankruptcy case. After dismissing the case, the bankrupt company's obligations before the creditors shall end and the bankrupt company shall resume its operations (Articles 32.2–32.4 of the Bankruptcy Law).

The court shall issue a decision to liquidate the bankrupt company considering it as insolvent on the following grounds (Articles 33 and 34 of the Bankruptcy Law):

(i)   if a request to recapitalize is not submitted,
(ii)   the court has not approved the recapitalization plan or the recapitalization plan has not been submitted to the court, and
(iii)   implementation of the recapitalization plan has become impossible.

Within 5 days of the date that the order to consider the bankrupt company insolvent and liquidate was issued, the court shall make a public announcement through the means of mass media. Within 5 days since the issuance of the court order to take under custody the bankrupt company's assets, the bankruptcy trustee shall take under custody the bankrupt company's assets and conduct the counting within 30 days.

The bankruptcy trustee shall distribute the bankrupt company's cash according to a cash distribution plan. The bankruptcy trustee shall submit to the court a cash distribution plan within 2 months of the issuance of the order to liquidate and shall provide a copy of the plan to all claimants. Considering real possibilities for selling the assets to be distributed, the court may extend, at the bankruptcy trustee's request, the cash distribution period (Article 35 of the Bankruptcy Law).

The court shall review the bankruptcy trustee's report and shall terminate the liquidation activities in the following circumstances (Article 36 of the Bankruptcy Law):

(i)   the creditors' claims were settled in full, or in the amount of assets in the bankrupt company's ownership, and no assets remain to be distributed; and
(ii)   all of the assets are not sold; however, the proceeds from the sold portion have satisfied the claim in full.

Immediately after the termination of the liquidation activities, the bankruptcy trustee shall inform the registering organization and remove the bankrupt company from the state register.

According to Article 87 of the Securities Market Law, the following circumstances shall be regarded as an emergency situation:

(i)   insolvency proceedings have been commenced against a regulated entity;
(ii)   circumstances have arisen that may lead to the liquidation of a regulated entity; and
(iii)   a competent authority has decided to reorganize a regulated entity on grounds specified in laws.

The FRC shall immediately take the following measures in the event of occurrence of an emergency situation, as per the law:

(i)   separate assets of the regulated entity from its financial reports and statements until such time that all claims of the clients have been satisfied;
(ii)   appoint a receiver for the regulated entity that is insolvent;

(iii)   change the management of a regulated entity, revoke the decisions made by the management, and restrict rights relating to disposal of cash or other property of the regulated entity; and

(iv)   restrict in full or in part, or suspend, the activities of the regulated entity.

U.   Event of Default and Cross-Default

There are no provisions for an event of default to be specified under the current regulations in Mongolia. Although the specific need to define events of default and possible cross-default provisions has not yet arisen, as there has been no case of default in the domestic bond market, it is expected that a clear definition of default and insolvency will be included in the future revisions of securities-market-related legislations.

In practice, corporate debt instruments issued in Mongolia are typically secured by a collateral or a guarantee by a third-party, as there are no instances of unsecured debt instruments issued in the past. A majority of these corporate debt securities are collateralized by either real estate assets or shares of the company, and the underwriters take it upon themselves to contract with the issuer via an underwriting agreement and a pledge agreement to repay investors' principal, interest, and undue loss payments with proceeds from the sale of collateral.

IV

Bond and Note Transactions and Trading Market Infrastructure

A. Trading of Debt Instruments

Publicly offered corporate debt instruments issued in Mongolia are listed and traded on an exchange, as required by the Securities Market Law. Government bonds issued prior to the temporary halt of government bond issuance in 2017 are traded on the BOM's interbank OTC trading platform for off-exchange issuances and through the MSE for the exchange issuances.

Particular market practices, the prevailing trading platforms, and mechanisms and other trading relevant practices are explained in detail in this chapter.

B. Trading Platforms

Publicly offered corporate debt securities can be listed and traded on either the government-owned MSE or the new privately owned MSX, which started its operations in 2015.

For government bonds, there are two trading platforms available: the MSE and the central bank's interbank OTC trading platform. These two trading platforms are operated separately, and a security traded on one cannot be traded on the other.

There is no dedicated marketplace for the secondary market trading of privately placed corporate debt instruments as these are legally not securities and are typically not registered at the central depository of securities. Typically, holders of these privately placed corporate debt instruments sign a tri-party purchase agreement including the issuer and the underwriter to purchase, and another purchase agreement to sell the debt instruments before its maturity. Since privately placed corporate debt instruments are typically issued with a maturity of 3–18 months, most investors tend to hold these debt instruments to maturity.

1. Trading on Mongolian Stock Exchange

In a typical bond market, bonds and notes tend to be traded in the OTC market. In the Mongolian bond market, however, publicly offered corporate debt securities and government bonds are all traded on the exchanges (MSE or MSX).

Government bonds started trading through the MSE in 1996 to commercial banks and individuals. These government bonds were offered irregularly, with short tenors, and only for the purpose of funding seasonal state budget shortages. Government Resolution No. 371 on 26 November 2014 approved the Regulation on Issuance and Trading of Government Securities, leading to government bonds being traded regularly on the MSE until the temporary halt in October 2017.

Publicly offered corporate debt securities started trading on the MSE in 2001, with the first corporate debt securities issued publicly through the exchange. Since then, over MNT24.5 billion has been raised through 15 corporate bond issuances from 13 companies (Figure 4.1).

Under the current regulatory requirements, only publicly offered corporate debt securities can be listed and traded on the exchange. An issuer is required to follow the requirements set by and receive approvals from both the MSE and FRC to be listed and publicly offer its securities. The MSCH handles the clearing and settlement of publicly offered corporate debt securities at the MSE.

**Figure 4.1: Secondary Market Trading Volumes
at the Mongolian Stock Exchange**
(MNT billion)

MNT = Mongolian togrog.
Sources: Financial Regulatory Commission and Mongolian Securities Clearing House.

In 2012, the MSE introduced the Millennium IT system to modernize the exchange's trading and settlement system, and started the process of converting to a T+2 settlement scheme. The FRC and the MSCH have completed the process of converting to a T+2 settlement cycle from the current prefunded settlement regime, and shifted to a delivery versus payment scheme starting from 31 March 2020.

Trading on the MSE occurs Monday through Friday unless the government declares a public holiday. The schedule of trading days for the year can be found on the MSE website. Daily trading hours are between 10:00 a.m. and 1:00 p.m. (Table 4.1).

Table 4.1: Trading Hours of the Mongolian Stock Exchange

Trading Session	Duration	Time
Opening auction	20 minutes	9:40 a.m.–10:00 a.m.
Normal trading session	3 hours	10:00 a.m.–1:00 p.m.
Closing price calculation	5 minutes	1:00 p.m.–1:05 p.m.

Source: Mongolian Stock Exchange. http://mse.mn/en/aboutus.

2.   Trading on the Mongol Securities Exchange

The Mongol Securities Exchange, a privately held securities exchange, was established in May 2015 and received its licenses to operate a regulated exchange in the securities market in July 2015.

The MSX is licensed to undertake securities trading as well as securities trading clearing, which are regulated activities under the Securities Market Law. The trading system of the MSX is provided by Nasdaq, Inc. It had 14 securities firms as trading members at the end of 2019.

As the newer securities exchange of Mongolia, the MSX had its first listing in November 2017. As of December 2019, the MSX had one company listed with a market capitalization of MNT2.5 billion, and one publicly offered corporate debt security listed. Secondary market trading volume for the MSX was MNT0.6 billion in 2018.

Due to the MSX having a license to undertake securities clearing operations, some of the more recent private placements of corporate debt instruments are using the exchange as the clearing and settlement agent. In 2019, there were three instances of an off-exchange issuance of corporate debt instruments through the MSX clearing system.

Trading on the MSX occurs Monday through Friday from 11:00 a.m. to 11:55 a.m. unless the government declares a public holiday (Table 4.2).

Table 4.2: Trading Hours of the Mongol Securities Exchange

Trading Session	Duration	Time
Opening auction	15 minutes	10:45 a.m.–11:00 a.m.
Market trading session	55 minutes	11:00 a.m.–11:55 a.m.
Closing price calculation	5 minutes	11:55 a.m.–12:00 noon

Source: Mongol Securities Exchange. https://www.msx.mn/menu-detail/14.

3.   Over-the-Counter Market

Currently, there is no regulated OTC market for corporate debt instruments. However, market participants such as the MASD and the exchanges are in the process of developing regulations to introduce an OTC marketplace for corporate debt instruments.

Under the previous 2014 Regulation on Issuance and Trading of Government Securities, secondary market trading for the off-exchange issuance of government bonds took place among commercial banks on the BOM interbank OTC trading platform. However, with the new 2019 Government Regulation on Primary and Secondary Market Operations of Domestic Government Securities, primary market issuance and secondary market trading of government securities are now regulated by this single regulation.

The central bank's OTC government bond market started trading in 2012, with Government Securities Issuing and Trading Regulation approved by Joint Order No. 217/A-161 by the MOF and the BOM, allowing for government bonds to trade regularly through the BOM's electronic trading system. The central bank's OTC market is regulated by the BOM and is only accessible by commercial banks, while bank customers can participate through their bank.

Secondary market trading of government bonds on the BOM interbank OTC market was stopped in February 2019, when the new Government Regulation on Primary and

Secondary Market Operations of Domestic Government Securities was approved. Prior to this, a total of MNT116.3 billion worth of government bond secondary market trading took place in the interbank OTC market in 2018, and MNT18.2 billion worth of government bond trading occurred in January 2019.

4.   Interbank Money Market

The BOM organizes and governs the interbank money market as part of its open market operation. The interbank money market started trading in 1993, with the BOM issuing the first CBBs in the market.

Market participants are so far limited to the central bank, commercial banks, the Development Bank of Mongolia, and the Deposit Insurance Corporation.

The key money market instruments traded on the interbank market are government and central bank securities repos, CBBs, overnight lending, and interbank deposits. Trades take place on the BOM interbank electronic trading system.

Transaction volume at the interbank market has picked up since 2018, following the temporarily halt of government bond issuance in October 2017 as a result of the EFF of the IMF. In 2017, total transaction volume on the interbank market was MNT7.7 trillion, which increased to MNT26.7 trillion in 2019.

C.   Mandatory Trade Reporting

The trading of publicly offered debt securities is conducted on the exchange trading systems, and trade reporting and monitoring is done by the exchanges and regulatory authorities.

Market participants (brokerage firms) are not required to disclose information on debt instruments trading on the exchanges after each trade but are required to send semiannual and annual financial reports to the monitoring department. In the case of block trades, trade counterparts are required to notify the exchange beforehand.

Settlement and clearing reports on publicly offered debt securities from the MSCH are sent to the FRC on a monthly basis, while the annual report is sent to the National Statistics Office. Settlement and clearing reports on exchange-traded government bonds are sent to the MOF on a monthly basis.

In addition, in accordance with the Regulation on Anti-Money Laundering and Terrorism Financing, information on any transactions above MNT20 million are delivered to the Bank of Mongolia.

For the government bonds that are traded on the central bank's interbank OTC market, results of secondary market trading are disclosed after each trading session on the BOM website.[34]

D.   Market Monitoring and Surveillance in the Secondary Market

The MSE works in close coordination with the FRC monitoring units to strengthen market surveillance, especially the monitoring of unusual transactions. Secondary market transactions at MSE are overseen by a monitoring program in accordance with

---

[34] BOM. Statistics. Result of Government Bond Auction.
https://www.mongolbank.mn/governmentbond.aspx?id=1_1.

the Monitoring and Surveillance Rules of the MSE. All securities trading is monitored by this program.

For the MSX, market monitoring and surveillance are conducted in accordance with the MSX Trading Rules.

E. Information on Debt Securities

Information on debt securities issued on the Mongolian bond market is publicly available and easily accessible online from the websites of policy bodies, regulatory authorities, and market institutions. Both professional and retail investors have many opportunities to obtain information on bonds and notes issued.

1. Ministry of Finance

Information on government securities are publicly available on the MOF website, which includes information such as government securities issuance schedules, auction results, as well as general information on the government securities issuance process.[35] Although the MOF website is translated into English, most information currently available is in the Mongolian language only.

2. Financial Regulatory Commission

The FRC issues a quarterly report with statistical data on the securities market, insurance market, non-banking financial market, and the commodities exchange market. The reports can be viewed or downloaded in PDF format directly from the FRC website.[36] There is no English translation provided currently.

3. Bank of Mongolia

The BOM publishes information on CBBs and government securities auctions on its website. Although the data are not real-time, data on auction results can be obtained from the BOM website.[37]

4. Mongolian Stock Exchange

The MSE provides comprehensive information on the securities traded at the exchange to the public on its website. In addition to securities transaction data, the website provides information on listed securities, as well as periodic reports and disclosure information. The MSE website also has information materials for investor education, relevant laws and regulations, and news on the listed securities.

Information on the latest announcement for debt securities can easily be viewed on the MSE website. Investors can find the latest announcements from either the news section or the new listing section of the website.

Information on listed debt securities can also be found on the MSE website at the listed companies section.[38] As there are no listed corporate debt securities currently available at the MSE, only information on government securities is shown.

---

[35] MOF. Securities. https://MOF.gov.mn/en/article/securities.
[36] FRC. Quarterly Summary of Financial Markets. http://www.frc.mn/d/pc/309.
[37] BOM. Government Securities Auction. https://www.mongolbank.mn/eng/governmentbond.aspx; and Central Bank Bills Auction. https://www.mongolbank.mn/eng/dblistcbb.aspx.
[38] MSE. Listed Securities. http://www.mse.mn/en/content/list/227; and Listed Government Securities. http://www.mse.mn/en/content/list/218.

The list of government bonds listed on the MSE shows information such as security code, coupon rate, face value, discounted price, trading date, and maturity dates, among other information. In the case of corporate bond issuances, the prospectus of the bond can be downloaded from the MSE website.

5. Mongol Securities Exchange

The MSX provides information on the securities traded on the exchange to the public on its website.[39] In addition to securities transactions, the website offers information on listed securities, exchange rules, and news on its listed securities.

F. Yields, Yield Curves, and Bond Indexes

The LCY government bond yield curve information can be found on the Bloomberg terminal. The BOM and MOF have published official LCY government bond yield curve information on the Bloomberg terminal since September 2015. It is accessible through the CRVF function by selecting "MNT Mongolian Govt Bond BVAL Yield Curve" under Mongolia, or by entering the code "GC BI1204."

Information on secondary market transactions for debt securities are disclosed on the MSE website. Currently, there are no corporate debt securities listed on the MSE and therefore only government bond trading information are visible on its website.[40]

However, since there are no new government bond exchange issuances planned at the moment and due to the lack of different maturity profiles of the existing exchange-traded government bonds, there are no bond indexes or yield curves calculated by the MSE.

G. Repo Market

1. Repo Market Overview

The money market is responsible for management and distribution of risk, cash, and other short-term financing sources among market participants. Currently, the interbank repo market in Mongolia is only available to commercial banks, and trades are conducted OTC directly between the banks and the BOM. Transfer of ownership is registered with the BOM for CBB repos, and with both the BOM and MCSD for government bond repos.

2. Repo Market Size

Interbank repo transaction volume has picked up since 2017, when the issuance of government securities was stopped temporarily. In addition, the BOM decreased the frequency and increased the maturity of CBB issuance beginning in April 2018, resulting in more secondary market trading activity in the interbank market. In 2016, the total volume of CBB repo trading was MNT1.2 trillion, comprising 13.5% of total interbank transactions, which increased to MNT6.5 trillion and 24.5% of total interbank transactions in 2019.

---

[39] MSX. Listed Companies. https://www.msx.mn/menu-detail/8.
[40] MSE. Government Securities Trading. http://www.mse.mn/en/exchange_government/224.

3.   Repo Practices in Mongolia

The BOM organizes and governs the repo market with its constituents as part of its open market operation and standing facilities with the banks. The relevant rules and regulations were updated in 2014 by the BOM through the Regulation on Central Bank Repo Financing and the Regulation on Central Bank Repo Transactions. The repo transactions follow the Domestic Repo Master Agreement developed by the BOM as the main contract for interbank transactions and for transactions between the BOM and banks.

CBBs and government bonds are allowed to be used as collateral in the repurchase agreements. Banks and the BOM use the BOM-developed Domestic Repo Master Agreement for their repo transactions. The transactions are recorded with both the MCSD and BOM for government bond repos, and with the BOM for CBB repos.

Market participants in the BOM interbank repo market are only the BOM and domestic commercial banks, as repos are a monetary policy tool of the BOM. Securities firms are not included, and direct access is not possible for nonresident investors. Parties interested in repo transactions will need to appoint a commercial bank to execute repo trades on their behalf.

H.   Securities Borrowing and Lending

Currently, there are no securities borrowing and lending activities in Mongolia.

I.   Government Bond Futures

Currently, there is no futures market in Mongolia.

Description of the Securities Settlement System

V

In 2003, the Settlement and Depository Department of the MSE was transformed into the MSCH Central Securities Depository. In 2016, the MSCH Central Securities Depository was divided into two companies, the MCSD and the MSCH by Resolution No. 147 of the Government of Mongolia.

The MCSD is responsible for the registration and safekeeping of securities, and the certificates of ownership of investors. Securities clearing and settlement is conducted by MSCH. The current settlement system is DVP with T+2.

Prior to the temporary cessation of government bond issuance in 2017, the MOF issued government bonds as per the Regulation on Issuance and Trading of Government Securities. Under this regulation, government bonds were issued through both off-exchange and exchange issuance methods. Off-exchange issuance was conducted through the BOM's interbank OTC market, while exchange issuance as a public offering was conducted through the MSE.

The clear separation of the interbank OTC government securities market and the public-offering exchange government securities market was a unique feature of the Mongolian market. Participation in the exchange market was open to anyone (including banks), while that of the interbank OTC market was limited to only banks. The different flows of issuance and trading on the two markets are shown in Figures 5.1 and 5.2.

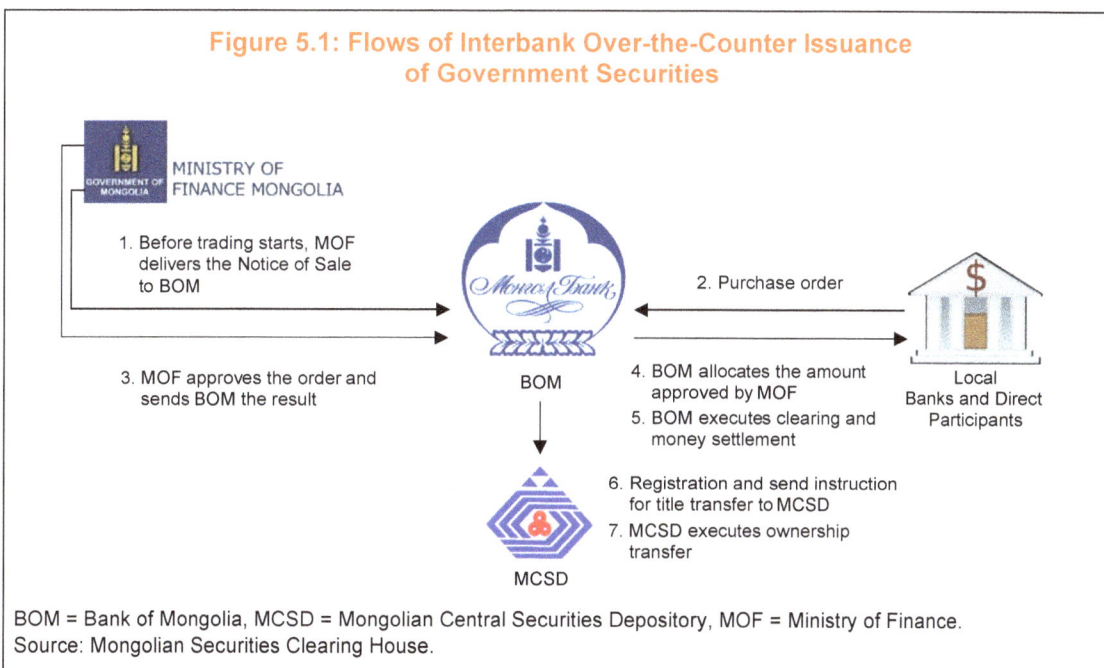

Figure 5.1: Flows of Interbank Over-the-Counter Issuance of Government Securities

MINISTRY OF FINANCE MONGOLIA

1. Before trading starts, MOF delivers the Notice of Sale to BOM

2. Purchase order

3. MOF approves the order and sends BOM the result

BOM

Local Banks and Direct Participants

4. BOM allocates the amount approved by MOF

5. BOM executes clearing and money settlement

6. Registration and send instruction for title transfer to MCSD

7. MCSD executes ownership transfer

MCSD

BOM = Bank of Mongolia, MCSD = Mongolian Central Securities Depository, MOF = Ministry of Finance.
Source: Mongolian Securities Clearing House.

Figure 5.2: Flows of Government Securities Issuance in the Exchange Market

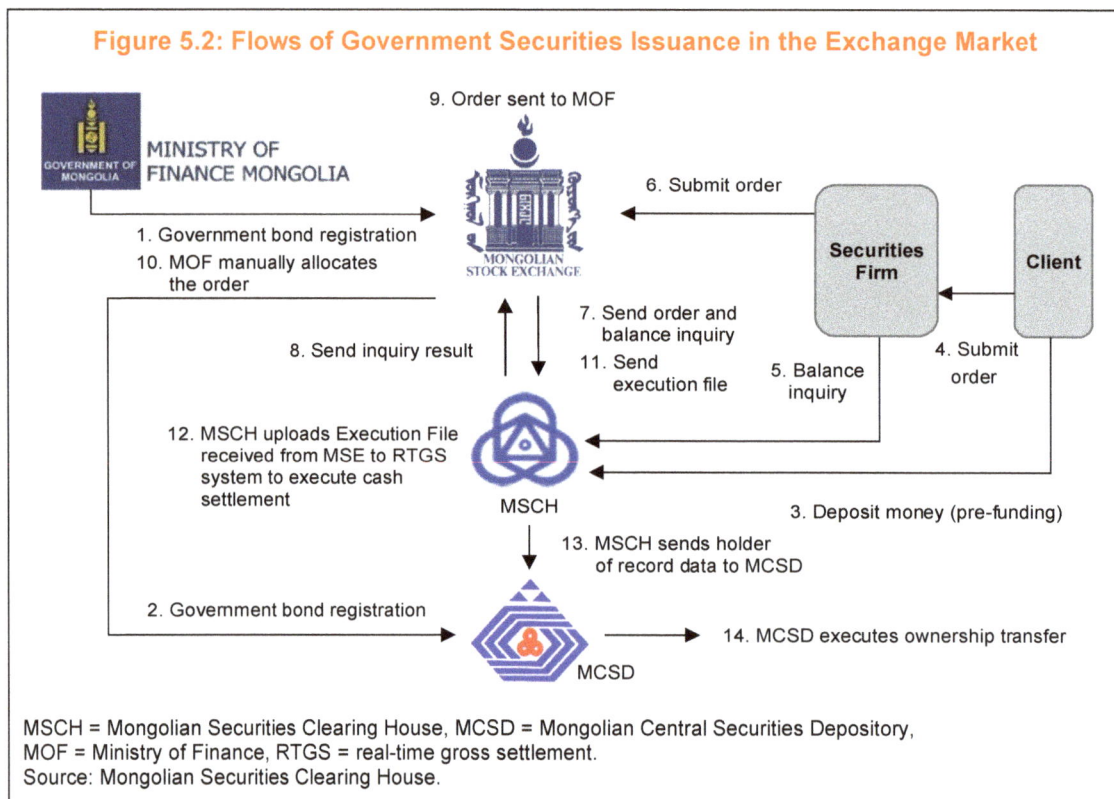

MSCH = Mongolian Securities Clearing House, MCSD = Mongolian Central Securities Depository,
MOF = Ministry of Finance, RTGS = real-time gross settlement.
Source: Mongolian Securities Clearing House.

Transactions involving government securities in the secondary market were separated based on the issuance scheme: if the securities were issued as a public offering through the exchange, the securities were traded through the exchange; and if the securities were issued to the interbank market, they were traded within interbank OTC transactions. The trade flows of government securities in the interbank OTC market and exchange market are shown in Figures 5.3 and 5.4.

Figure 5.3: Trade Flows of Government Securities in the Interbank Over-the-Counter Market

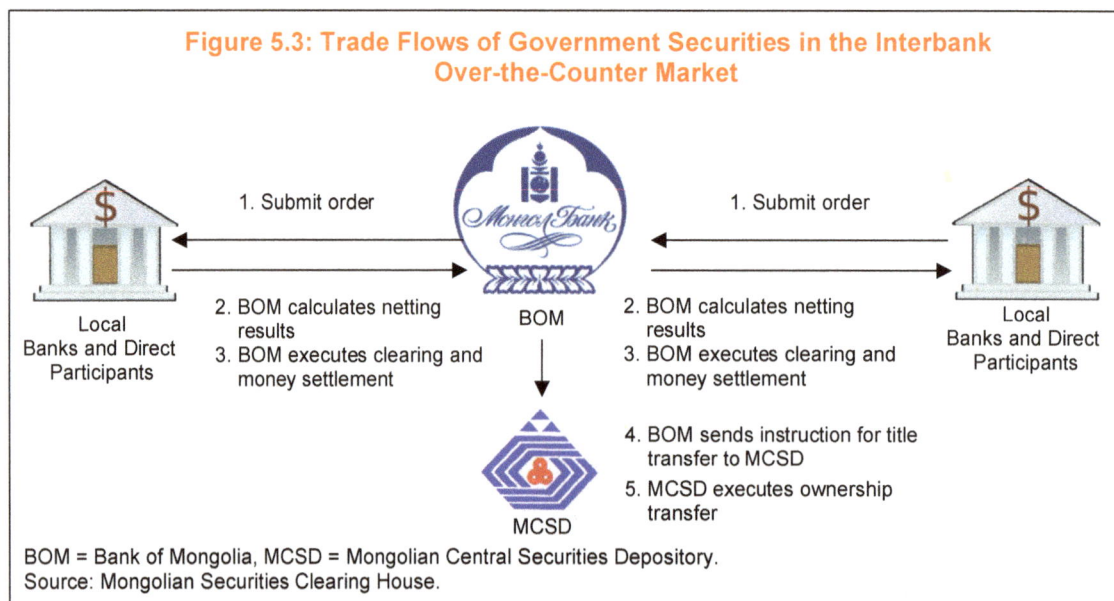

BOM = Bank of Mongolia, MCSD = Mongolian Central Securities Depository.
Source: Mongolian Securities Clearing House.

Figure 5.4: Trade Flows of Government Securities in the Exchange Market

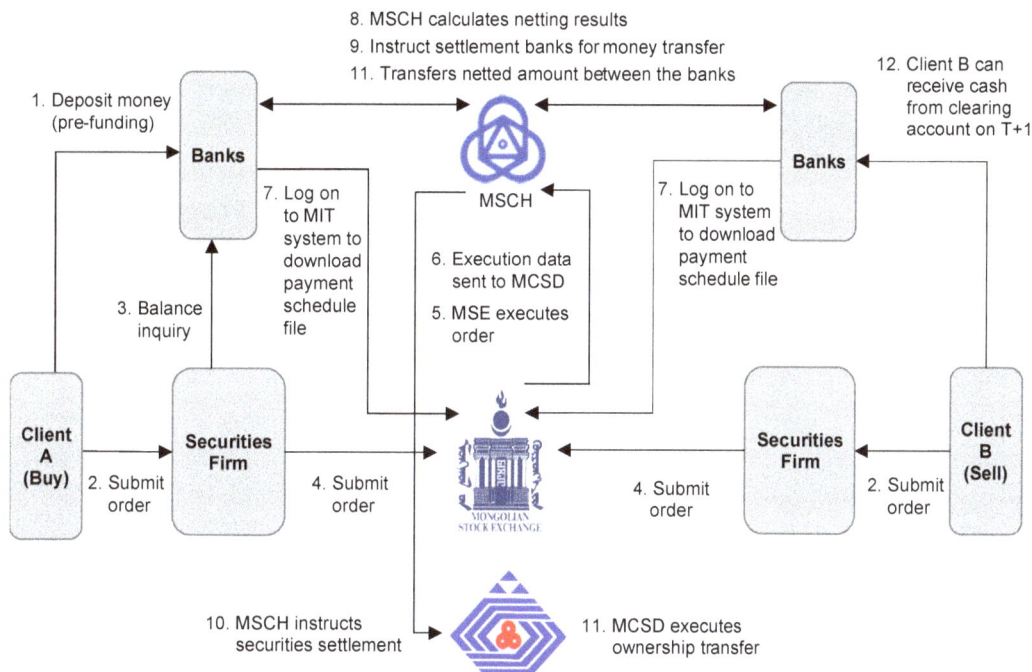

8. MSCH calculates netting results
9. Instruct settlement banks for money transfer
11. Transfers netted amount between the banks

1. Deposit money (pre-funding)

Banks

12. Client B can receive cash from clearing account on T+1

7. Log on to MIT system to download payment schedule file

MSCH

7. Log on to MIT system to download payment schedule file

Banks

3. Balance inquiry

6. Execution data sent to MCSD

5. MSE executes order

Client A (Buy)

2. Submit order

Securities Firm

4. Submit order

4. Submit order

Securities Firm

2. Submit order

Client B (Sell)

10. MSCH instructs securities settlement

11. MCSD executes ownership transfer

MSCH = Mongolian Securities Clearing House, MCSD = Mongolian Central Securities Depository,
MIT = Millennium IT System.
Source: Mongolian Securities Clearing House.

Interest and principal payments of government bonds are conducted as shown in Figures 5.5 and 5.6.

Figure 5.5: Coupon Payment and Redemption Flows of Government Securities in the Interbank Over-the-Counter Market

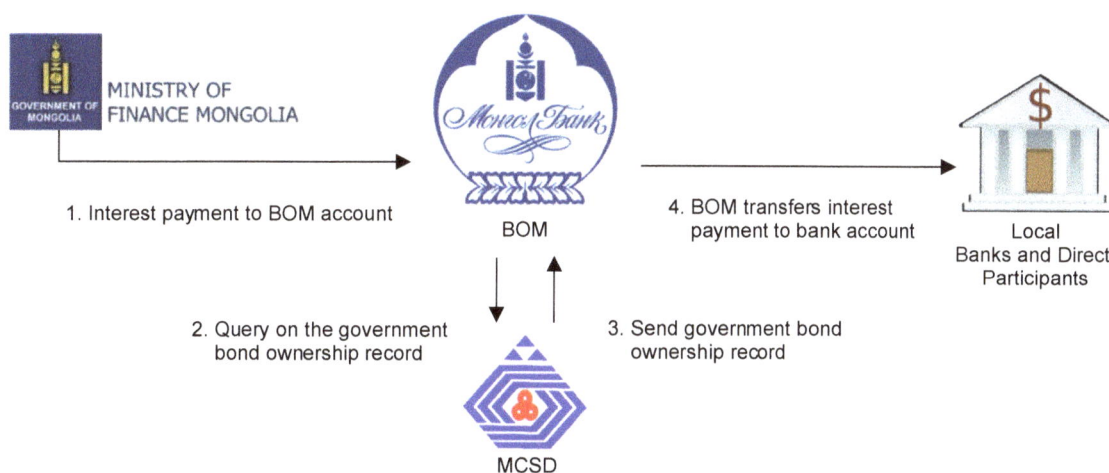

MINISTRY OF FINANCE MONGOLIA

1. Interest payment to BOM account

BOM

4. BOM transfers interest payment to bank account

Local Banks and Direct Participants

2. Query on the government bond ownership record

3. Send government bond ownership record

MCSD

BOM = Bank of Mongolia, MCSD = Mongolian Central Securities Depository.
Source: Mongolian Securities Clearing House.

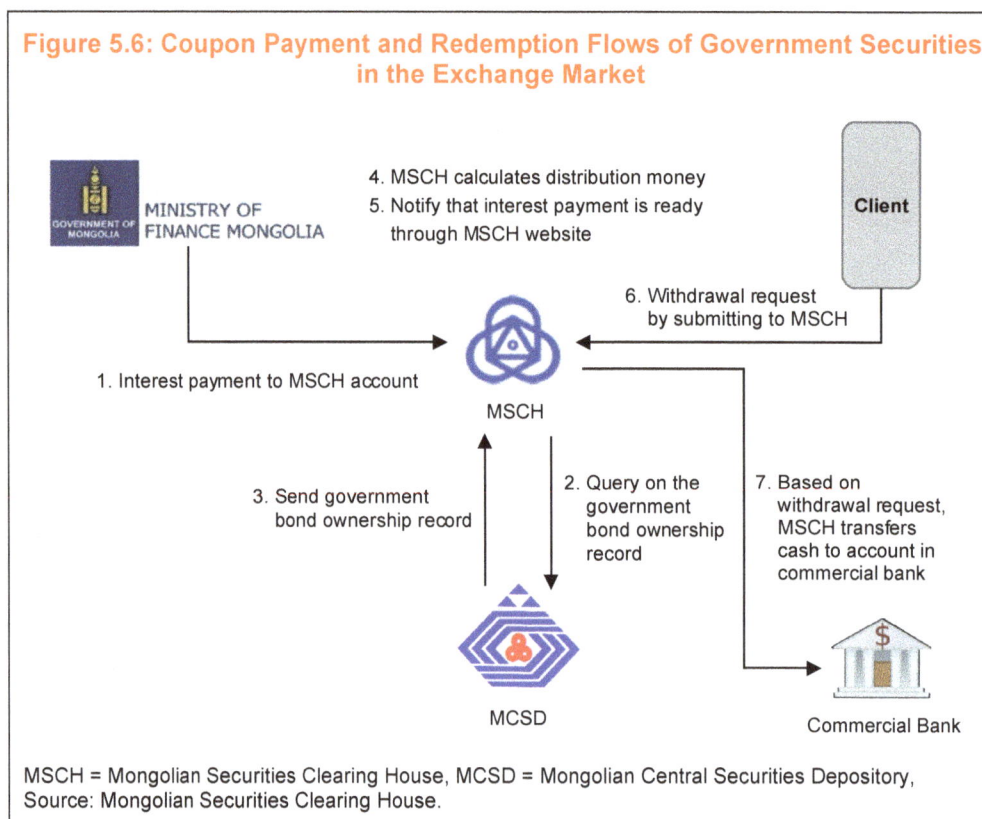

Figure 5.6: Coupon Payment and Redemption Flows of Government Securities in the Exchange Market

MSCH = Mongolian Securities Clearing House, MCSD = Mongolian Central Securities Depository,
Source: Mongolian Securities Clearing House.

Primary and secondary market settlement flows of publicly offered corporate debt securities are the same as that of MSE-traded government securities.

The International Securities Identification Number (ISIN) standard security identification has been used in the Mongolian capital market since January 2013. An ISIN is assigned by the MCSD and sent regularly to the Association of National Numbering Agencies. The country code of Mongolia is "MN."

Table 5.1 includes examples of ISINs for Mongolian securities.

Table 5.1: Examples of International Securities Identification Numbers in Mongolia

Debt Securities Type	ISIN
Short-term government securities	MNZGKHB13000
Long-term government securities	MN0ZGEB13018
Publicly offered corporate debt securities (Suu bond)	MN0SUUB30154
Listed stocks (Suu joint stock company)	MN00SUU01355

ISIN = International Securities Identification Number.
Source: Mongolian Central Securities Depository.

Under the General Directive on Developing Economy and Society of Mongolia in 2020, approved by the Parliament in May 2019, the FRC introduced delivery versus payment (DVP) settlement into the Mongolian capital market to update the securities settlement system to international standards. Under the FRC Resolution No. 29 of 29 January 2020, Mongolia adopted the DVP with T+2 finality arrangement starting from 31 March 2020. As a result, this chapter will be updated with these changes in future revisions of this guide.

VI

Bond Market Costs and Taxation

This chapter details the typical costs incurred by issuers and investors in the Mongolian bond market, with an emphasis on costs associated with publicly offered debt securities issuance and settlement.

For ease of reference, the descriptions of the types of costs are given in the context of the actions to be taken by issuers or investors (as explained in this document) and follow the life cycle of publicly offered debt securities in the Mongolian bond market.

A.   Costs Associated with Debt Securities Issuance

Under the Securities Market Law, any securities issuance offered to 50 or more investors is deemed a public offering and is required to comply with the relevant requirements. When offering securities to the public, the issuer is required to appoint a licensed underwriter in addition to licensed securities service providers.

1.   Registration of Bond Issuance and Approval from the Financial Regulatory Commission (Mandatory for Public Offers)

Issuers intending to offer debt securities via a public offering in Mongolia are required to file a request along with a securities prospectus with the FRC. The issuer in required to pay a one-time fixed fee of MNT500,000 to the FRC to process and review the request. The service fee is nonrefundable and is required to be paid before the application to the FRC, as the Securities Market Law requires that a document evidencing payment of the regulatory service fee be appended to the application to register securities.

2.   National Stamp Duty

A national stamp duty of MNT100,000 is required by the State Registration Office for processing the request at the FRC. The stamp duty is levied on legal entities for receiving services from state authorities in accordance with the Law on National Stamp Duty. The stamp duty is nonrefundable and is paid before the application to the FRC, as a document evidencing payment of the regulatory service fee is required to be appended to the application to register securities.

3.   Underwriter Fee

According to the Securities Market Law, corporate debt instrument issuance does not require underwriters, unlike equity. However, due to a lack of expertise, knowledge, and client base, corporates typically appoint underwriters when issuing debt instruments for public offer. The underwriters are tasked with compiling the necessary documents and the securities prospectus for issuance, as well as issuing an independent opinion on the securities offered.

An underwriter will charge a fee that is typically commensurate with the effort and risk of taking over part or all of the debt securities issuance from the issuer and the total fee amount is subject to negotiations between issuer and underwriter.

4.   Advisory Fees

The Securities Market Law requires that any securities issued to the public have third-party opinions on the issuance from an FRC-licensed legal firm and auditing firm. These advisors are required to have a license from the FRC to operate in the capital market.

There is no distinction between the requirements for publicly offered debt securities and other types of securities in the Securities Market Law. Under the law, the securities prospectus is required to include legal and audit opinions, and property valuation reports prepared by third-party advisors. As such, the issuer is required to appoint a valuation firm to prepare a property valuation report of the company assets. An asset valuation firm is an entity that provides property valuation and appraisal services under a special license. Typically, these firms provide asset valuation for the purposes of valuing collateral assets and asset appraisal for insurance purposes. For an asset valuation firm to provide valuation services to participants in the securities market, which is considered a regulated activity by law, it is required to be licensed by the FRC. In the context of the securities market, asset valuation firms provide a valuation report on properties and assets on the issuer's balance sheet, as well as a business valuation report of the issuer as an enterprise. These requirements are specific to the Mongolian capital market and to the public offering of securities in general.

The advisors charge the issuer service fees in relation to their services provided and the total fee amount is subject to negotiations between issuer and advisors.

5.   Mongolian Central Securities Depository Fee

Under the Securities Market Law, all securities offered on the public market are required to be deposited at the MCSD, including government bonds and publicly offered debt securities. The securities are registered and deposited at the MCSD upon approval by the FRC.

A one-time fee of 0.045% of the total issuance amount is charged for depositing corporate debt instruments at the MCSD, regardless of the duration. There are no recurring fees payable to the MCSD. Government bonds do not incur the depository fee with the MCSD, although they are registered and deposited at the central depository.

B.   Costs Associated with Debt Securities Listing

Publicly offered securities, including publicly offered corporate debt securities, are required to be listed on an exchange. Issuers may list their debt securities on either the MSE or MSX. A listing on the exchange is subject to the review and approval of both the FRC and the exchange, and incurs a number of fees, both one-time and recurring.

In addition to professional service fees and FRC fees, the debt securities issuer is required to pay a securities registration application fee and a registration service fee to the exchange.

For a publicly offered corporate debt securities listing on the exchange, the issuer is required to pay the fees outlined below.

1.   Initial Listing Review Fees

The issuer is required to pay a one-time fee of MNT2 million to the MSE for the listing application review of the securities for public offer. This listing review fee is nonrefundable.

For the MSX, there are no fees for an initial listing review.

2.   Initial Listing Registration Fees

The issuer is required to pay a one-time fee of 0.1% of the issuance amount for publicly offered corporate debt securities and 0.025% for government debt securities to register them at the MSE. The minimum required registration fee amount is MNT2.5 million at the MSE.

The initial listing registration fees for the MSX is 0.1% of the issuance amount for publicly offered corporate debt securities.

3.   Initial Listing Trading Fees

For sellers of debt securities on the primary market, the MSE charges government debt securities a trading fee of 0.12% and publicly offered debt securities 0.1575% of the total issuance amount.

The MSX charges sellers of publicly offered corporate debt securities a fee of 0.2%.

4.   Initial Listing Clearing and Settlement Fees

For sellers of debt securities on the primary market, the MSCH charges government bonds a clearing and settlement fee of 0.00175% and publicly offered corporate debt securities 0.0075% of the total issuance amount.

5.   Annual Listing Management Fees

There is no annual recurring listing management fee for publicly offered debt securities at the MSE, MSX, or MCSD.

6.   Change in Registration and Delisting Fees

The issuer is required to pay a one-time fee of MNT1.5 million to the MSE to make changes to the registration of the listed securities or to delist them. The MSX has not set fees for changes in the registration of listed securities.

C.   Ongoing Costs for Issuers of Securities

Ongoing costs arise from service providers appointed by the issuer for the provision of services throughout the lifecycle of the publicly offered debt securities. These services typically include the representative of bondholders' function.

1.   Fee for Representative or Trustee of Bondholders

There are three custodian banks operating in Mongolia licensed by the FRC. The fees charged by these custodian banks are subject to negotiations with each of the banks.

The concept of bondholders' representative or bond trustee is not present in Mongolia under the current legislation. To introduce the concept in Mongolia, the Company Law needs to be amended. A revised law is currently under discussion among the regulators. It is expected that the concept of bond trustee will be introduced in the future revision of the Company Law.

D. Costs for Deposit and Withdrawal of Securities

Publicly offered debt securities, including government bonds, are dematerialized and deposited at the MCSD under the Securities Market Law. There are no fees related to deposits and withdrawals for government securities, while a one-time initial securities registration fee is charged for other types of debt instruments at the MCSD. The fee is paid by the issuer.

There are no recurring deposit fees and withdrawal fees at the MCSD.

E. Costs Associated with Securities Trading

Publicly offered corporate debt securities issued in the Mongolian market are required to be listed and traded on the exchange. Exchange issuances of government bonds are listed and traded on the MSE. The fees applicable to debt instrument transactions differ between these two types of debt instruments.

1. Exchange Trades

Investors trade in publicly offered debt instruments on the exchange by submitting an order via brokerage firms, which are members of the exchanges.

a. Brokerage Fee (investor pays to securities firm)

A securities firm may levy brokerage fees on investors for trading publicly offered debt instruments on the exchange. These fees may differ from broker to broker and are subject to negotiations with the respective investor. Typically, an investor pays a single brokerage fee to the securities firm for the securities trade, and the securities firm pays the trading, clearing, and settlement fees to the respective agencies from the brokerage fee paid by the investor. As of 2019, these brokerage fees were in the range of 1.48%–3.00% for all brokerage firms.

b. Trading Fee (securities firm pays to the exchange)

Trading fees on the exchange differ for government bonds and publicly offered corporate debt securities, and are payable by the brokerage firm to the exchange. In addition, fees for primary market issuance and secondary market trading are different for buyers and sellers of the bonds.

i. Government bonds

On the MSE, for the purchase of government bonds on the primary market, a 0.00875% fee is levied on the total purchase amount. For secondary market trading, the buyer is charged a 0.00875% fee on the total purchase amount, while the seller is not required to pay any fees.

Government securities are not traded on the MSX.

ii.   Publicly listed corporate debt securities

On the MSE, for the purchase of publicly offered corporate debt securities on the primary market, a 0.0175% fee is levied on the total purchase amount. For secondary market trading, the buyer is charged a 0.0175% fee on the total purchase amount, while the seller is not required to pay any fees.

For the MSX, the buyer is charged a 0.1% fee on the total purchase amount, while the seller is charged a 0.2% fee in both the primary and secondary markets.

c.   Clearing and Settlement Fee (securities firm pays to the MSCH)

Clearing and settlement fees at the MSCH differ for government bonds and publicly offered corporate debt securities, and are payable by the brokerage firm to the MSCH. In addition, fees are different for buyers and sellers of government bonds.

i.   Government bonds

For the purchase of government bonds on the primary market, a 0.00375% fee is levied on the total purchase amount. For secondary market trading, the buyer is charged a 0.00375% fee on the total purchase amount, while the seller is charged a 0.00175% fee on the total selling amount.

ii.   Publicly listed corporate debt securities

For the purchase of publicly offered corporate debt securities, a 0.0075% fee is levied on the total purchase amount, while the seller is charged a 0.0075% fee on the total selling amount. Both primary market participants and secondary market participants are charged the same amount for publicly offered corporate debt securities.

The summary of government bond trading fees is outlined in Table 6.1 and of publicly offered corporate debt securities trading fees in Table 6.2.

Table 6.1: Government Bond Trading Fees

Government Bond	MSE		MSCH		Broker	
	Buyer (%)	Seller (%)	Buyer (%)	Seller (%)	Buyer	Seller
Primary market	0.00875	0.12000	0.00375	0.00175	Contract	Contract
Secondary market	0.00875	0.00000	0.00375	0.00175	Contract	Contract

MSE = Mongolian Stock Exchange, MSCH = Mongolian Securities Clearing House.
Sources: MSE, MSCH, and Mongolian Central Securities Depository.

Table 6.2: Publicly Listed Corporate Debt Security Trading Fees

Corporate Bond	MSE		MSX		MSCH		Broker	
	Buyer (%)	Seller (%)	Buyer (%)	Seller (%)	Buyer (%)	Seller (%)	Buyer	Seller
Primary market	0.0175	0.0175	0.1	0.2	0.0075	0.0075	Contract	Contract
Secondary market	0.0175	0.0000	0.1	0.2	0.0075	0.0075	Contract	Contract

MSE = Mongolian Stock Exchange, MSX = Mongol Securities Exchange, MSCH = Mongolian Securities Clearing House.
Sources: MSE, MSX, MSCH, and Mongolian Central Securities Depository.

2.   Bank Fees

In addition to the trading, settlement, and clearing fees, bank transaction fees may be levied on the transferring party. For domestic interbank transfers, MNT500 is typically charged from the transferring party.

F.   Costs for Safekeeping, Settlement, and Transfer of Bonds and Notes

There are currently three custodian banks operating in Mongolia licensed by the FRC. The fees charged by these custodian banks are subject to negotiations with each of the banks. An investor is not required to pay deposit fees and withdrawal fees at the MCSD. However, if the investor wishes to appoint a custodian bank for safekeeping of securities, they may do so at their own expense.

G.   Fees Related to Securities Borrowing and Lending Transactions

Currently there are no securities borrowing and lending activities in Mongolia.

H.   Taxation Framework and Requirements

1.   General Overview

Taxes in Mongolia comprise taxes, fees, and payments in accordance with the General Tax Law. Tax policy is within the mandate of the MOF. Tax collection, registration, and oversight is implemented by the General Taxation Authority.

Incomes earned from securities and debt instruments are taxed in accordance with the Corporate Income Tax Law and the Personal Income Tax Law.

2.   Duties and Taxes on Debt Instruments

According to the General Taxation Law (amended 22 March 2019), dividends and interest and rental income are subject to Mongolian personal income tax at the flat rate of 10% for residents and a 20% withholding tax for the Mongolian-sourced income of nonresidents, unless the term is reduced pursuant to an applicable tax treaty. Typically, the local bank retains 20% of these interest payments sent abroad and remits to the Tax Authority of Mongolia.

Government bonds and debt instruments issued by the Development Bank of Mongolia are exempt from income tax under the current tax legislation. In addition, under the revised Corporate Income Tax Law and Personal Income Tax Law (effective

1 January 2020), interest income earned from publicly offered corporate debt securities are subject to a 5% income tax, instead of 10%.

Capital gains from the trading of publicly offered corporate debt securities are subject to the standard tax rate of 10% in principle, but the market practice needs to be referred to the local custodian.

Typically, investors can choose to report, pay, and finalize applicable taxes with the General Taxation Authority either directly or through the securities brokerage firm.

Table 6.3 provides an overview of the tax regime for investors in Mongolian government bonds and corporate debt instruments. Details and the application of the individual types of tax are explained in the subsequent sections.

Table 6.3: Duties and Taxes on Debt Instruments

Duties and Tax	Type of Debt Instruments	Tax Rate
Personal Income Tax	Government bonds	Exempt
	Publicly offered corporate debt instruments	5%
	Privately placed corporate debt instruments	10%
Corporate Income Tax	Government bonds	Exempt
	Publicly offered corporate debt instruments	5%
	Privately placed corporate debt instruments	10%
Withholding Tax	Government bonds	Exempt
	Corporate debt instruments	20%
Capital Gains Tax	Government bonds	10%
	Corporate debt instruments	10%
Stamp Duty		
Value-Added Tax		

Source: Ministry of Finance.

3.   Corporate Income Tax

There are three types of corporate income taxes: income from operations, capital gains, and income from assets under the Corporate Income Tax Law. Income from the sale of securities is considered income from operations, while interest income is considered income from assets.

Interest income on debt instruments issued by the Government of Mongolia and the Development Bank of Mongolia is exempt from tax, while interest income earned from publicly offered corporate debt securities and dividend income earned from publicly listed securities is subject to a 5% income tax, instead of 10%.

For nonresidents, a 20% withholding tax is levied on Mongolian-sourced income, unless the term is reduced pursuant to an applicable tax treaty. Taxes on corporate income shall be levied based on the following table for residents and nonresidents.

Table 6.4: Corporate Income Tax for Residents and Nonresidents

Taxpayer	Taxable Income	Tax Rate	
Resident	Income from operations, capital gains	For income up to MNT6.0 billion	10%
		For income above MNT6.0 billion	MNT600 million plus 25% on income above MNT6.0 billion
	Interest income, dividend income	10% (Government bonds 0%, Publicly offered corporate debt instruments 5%)	
Nonresident	Profit transferred abroad from representative office of a foreign entity	20%	
	Income earned and originated in Mongolia		
	Interest income attributable to a nonresident taxpayer from bonds issued by a Mongolian commercial bank on domestic and international securities exchanges	5%	

MNT = Mongolian togrog.
Source: Government of Mongolia, Ministry of Finance.

4. Withholding Tax

The Corporate Income Tax Law also specifies the tax on income earned by foreign investors from Mongolia. A 20% tax is imposed on income earned from operating in Mongolia and the following revenues originating in Mongolia:

(i) dividend income from business entities registered in Mongolia;
(ii) interest and guarantee payments;
(iii) income from royalties, interest on financial leases, payments to management expenses, lease payments, and income from lease of tangible and intangible assets;
(iv) income from goods sold, work performed, and services rendered in the territory of Mongolia; and
(v) income from work and services earned directly or electronically from Mongolia.

If a foreign entity issues debt securities in Mongolia, it is not clear whether the tax on the proceeds is attributable to withholding tax.

Although dividends and interest paid to foreign investors are subject to a 20% withholding tax, countries included in the Double Tax Treaty with Mongolia are subject to a lower tax rate.

5. Capital Gains Tax

Although there is no income category related to capital gains or income attributable to an increase in asset value in the Mongolian tax system, income earned from the sale of securities is taxed. The tax rate levied for capital gains is same as the corporate income tax.

To determine the taxable income from sale of securities, the initial purchasing price, and the fees related to the purchase are deducted from the sale price. This provision does not apply to sale of securities issued by the entity itself.

However, market practice needs to be referred to the local custodian regarding the calculation of incomes attributable to a capital gains tax.

6. Stamp Duty

Foreign and domestic residents and legal entities pay stamp duty on services such as certifying contracts and ownership of securities on paper (MNT5,000) in Mongolia. Although there is no stamp duty charged on services related to investing and purchasing securities, a stamp duty of MNT13,000–MNT1,800,000 (for opening a representative office for foreign-owned banks) is charged based on the type of services received, such as registering a new legal entity, representative office, or obtaining a license to conduct regulated operations in the securities market in Mongolia.

Stamp duty is levied on legal entities for receiving services from state authorities in accordance with the Law on National Stamp Duty. The list of state services that require national stamp duties to be paid can be found in the law.

Generally, obtaining licenses and registering patents and ownership rights that result in a form of paper certificates are required to pay stamp duties. Stamp duty will not be paid for book-entry securities trading.

7. Value-Added Tax

Issuing, transferring, selling, receiving, and providing guarantees on securities are exempt from value-added tax in Mongolia.

8. Double Taxation Agreements

Double taxation agreements are treaties signed by the Government of Mongolia with other countries that specify tax exemption on income derived from investments so that investors are only liable to pay income tax in one country as a means of inducing foreign investment.

As of 2019, 26 countries have entered the Agreement for the Avoidance of Double Taxation and the Prevention of Fiscal Evasion with respect to Taxes on Income and on Capital with the Government of Mongolia. The full list of countries with tax treaties can be viewed on the Mongolian Tax Authority website (Mongolian language only).[41] English readers can find the unofficial list from websites of one of the big four accounting firms with offices in Mongolia.[42]

9. Tax Concessions or Exemptions for Nonresident Investors

There are no tax concessions specifically for nonresident investors in the securities market, other than those available under existing double taxation agreements.

10. Tax Treatment of Investment Funds

Income from investment funds is tax exempt in Mongolia. Incomes earned from investing in investment funds are not tax exempt under the current legislation. However, market practice needs to be referred to the local custodian or legal advisor.

---

[41] Mongolian Tax Authority. Tax Treaties. http://www.mta.mn/c/view/11957.
[42] PricewaterhouseCoopers, LLP. Mongolia. Individual–Foreign Tax Relief and Tax Treaties. http://taxsummaries.pwc.com/ID/Mongolia-Individual-Foreign-tax-relief-and-tax-treaties.

11. Updates on the Tax Law

The Parliament approved a revision to its existing General Taxation Law on 22 March 2019, which introduced various tax reductions to promote the bond market and the domestic capital market in general. The new Tax Law came into effect on 1 January 2020.

The details of the changes under the new Tax Law are outlined in Chapter X.A.

VII

Market Size and Statistics

Since the Bond Market Guide for Mongolia is most likely to be updated only on a biennial basis, it is not the best channel for the dissemination of market statistics. Hence, instead of bond market statistics, a list of recommended sources for detailed, accurate, and current information sources on the Mongolian bond market is provided here. These sources are listed below in alphabetical order. However, some of the information are available in the Mongolian language only.

- Bank of Mongolia
  Statistical Publications and Reports
  https://www.mongolbank.mn/eng/liststatistic.aspx

  Monthly Statistical Bulletin (latest version issued on December 2019)
  https://www.mongolbank.mn/documents/statistic/2019/12.pdf

- Financial Regulatory Commission
  Market Data (only available in Mongolian)
  http://www.frc.mn/d/s/2

  Quarterly Summary of Financial Markets (only available in Mongolian)
  http://www.frc.mn/d/pc/309

- Ministry of Finance
  Securities Issuance—Schedules, Statements, and Results (only available in Mongolian)
  https://MOF.gov.mn/en/article/securities

- Mongol Securities Exchange
  Listed Securities (only available in Mongolian)
  https://www.msx.mn/menu-detail/8

- Mongolian Stock Exchange
  Daily Trading Summary (summary reports accessible from the Trade Reports section on the left side of page)
  http://mse.mn/en/trade_today/23

  Monthly Trading Summary (latest version, as of December 2019)
  http://mse.mn/uploads/ariljaa/reports/report_en-18.pdf

  Annual Trading Summary 2019 (latest version only available in Mongolian)
  http://mse.mn/uploads/ariljaa/reports/report_mn-14.pdf

- National Statistics Office
  Social and Economic Situation of Mongolia (monthly)
  http://www.en.nso.mn/contents/2

VIII

Presence of
an Islamic Bond Market

At present, there is no Islamic bond market in Mongolia.

IX

Mongolian Bond Market Challenges and Opportunities

This chapter discusses some of the current and ongoing challenges for the Mongolian bond market and its participants and describes the market developments being undertaken by the regulators and market participants that could address these challenges.

A.   Challenges in the Mongolian Bond Market

1.   Segregation of Debt Instrument Requirements

As the development of the Mongolian bond market is in its early stage, there are not many pieces of legislation or regulations targeted specifically to the bond market. Under the current regulations, no distinctions are made on requirements for debt instruments and other types of securities such as equities. As such, stringent requirements typically applied to public companies and initial public offerings (IPOs) are also applied to publicly offered debt instruments.

Under the Securities Market Law and related regulations, publicly offered securities are required to get approval from the FRC and the exchange, which can take many months, for each issuance regardless of the type of security. In addition, a securities prospectus required for public offering needs to include an audited financial report, a legal opinion, as well as an asset valuation report prepared by a licensed valuation firm, which is a unique feature in Mongolia. These requirements intended for public companies conducting an IPO add to the cost and time required for publicly offering debt instruments in the Mongolian market. However, it is expected that these issues will be addressed in future amendments to existing legislation.

2.   Regulatory Framework for Privately Placed Debt Instruments

Under the current regulations, privately placed corporate debt instruments are outside the scope of the Securities Market Law, and not considered as security unless it is registered at a regulated securities depository entity (MCSD or custodian). Current prevailing market practice for corporate debt instrument issuance is private placement in the form of loan agreements between the issuer, underwriter, and investor. Although these are loan agreements legally, they are considered as corporate bonds in the Mongolian local market and tend to be marketed under the name "bonds."

One of the key reasons for such practice is because of the lengthy process and costs required with public offering of corporate debt instruments, as explained earlier. Another reason is the absence of a regulatory framework for private placements, as the Securities Market Law is only applicable to the public offering of securities. This unregulated market is a source of major concern for regulators and market participants, as a single default instance on one of these privately placed debt instruments may result in erosion of trust in the Mongolian bond market and the capital market as a whole. However, to resolve this issue, market participants and the regulators are making efforts to prepare necessary revisions of the relevant regulations.

3. Unsecured Debt Instruments

Prevailing market practice when issuing corporate debt instruments in Mongolia is to guarantee the repayment with collateral or third-party guarantees, regardless of whether they are privately placed or publicly offered debt instruments. Although it is not strictly required under the current regulations, regulators tend to ask for repayment guarantees from the issuer when approving public offering of corporate debt instruments.

Part of the reason for this is the absence of credit rating agencies or credit guarantee institutions in the Mongolian bond market. However, the major contributing factor is the lack of professional institutional investors in the market. Retail investors are the primary participants in the corporate bond market in Mongolia, and because the key factor driving retail investors to participate in the bond market is the higher interest rate of corporate debt instruments compared to bank deposits. As a result, retail investors tend to compare these debt instruments to the safety of bank deposits, and ask for a guarantee on the repayments of these debt instruments. In addition, corporate debt instruments being issued in Mongolia have shorter maturities, typically 3–18 months.

Efforts from both market participants as well as the regulators are necessary to address this issue, in addition to efforts to drive the development of a professional investor segment in the Mongolian capital market, including pension funds and insurance companies.

4. Bankruptcy Definition

The current legal framework provides no clear definition regarding provisions on an event of default, although the specific need to define events of default and possible cross-default provisions has not yet arisen, as there were no cases of default in the local bond market. However, it is expected that default and insolvency will be clearly defined in future revisions of securities market legislation.

5. Developing an Institutional or Professional Investor Segment, and Increasing Participation of High-Net-Worth Individuals

One of the key challenges facing bond market development in Mongolia is the lack of professional investor or institutional investor participation in the corporate bond market. As a result, retail investors are the primary participants in the corporate bond market, leading to shorter maturities and the need for secured or collateralized issuance of corporate debt instruments. With a lack of professional investors, it is also difficult to develop an OTC marketplace for corporate debt instruments.

To increase the participation of professional investors in the Mongolian capital market, several revisions are required in current regulations, including the loosening of tight restrictions, placing limits on investable asset classes for insurance companies and investment funds, and promoting reform to allow the Social Security Fund to invest in the local capital market.

Professional investors are defined under the current regulations as entities or persons engaged in professional investment activity, such as investment funds, pension funds, banks, and entities licensed to undertake activities related to NBFI activities, insurance, underwriting or dealer activities, or other entities or persons authorized, either by law or the FRC, to conduct professional investment activities. However, there is no definition of a high-net-worth individual in the current regulations in Mongolia, which needs to be defined in future revisions to capital market regulations.

B.   Opportunities in the Mongolian Bond Market

In addition to efforts being made by market participants and regulators to address the challenges mentioned in the previous section, several developments are providing additional opportunities in the Mongolian bond market.

1.   International Monetary Fund Extended Fund Facility Program Completion

The IMF approved a 3-year arrangement under the EFF on 24 May 2017 to support Mongolia's economic reform program after a sharp decline of commodity prices and a slowdown in key export markets. The total USD5.5 billion IMF-led financing package included programs aimed at fiscal consolidation, reducing pressure on domestic financial markets, stabilizing the external position, restoring debt sustainability, rehabilitating the banking system and strengthening the BOM, as well as a broad set of structural reforms, according to the IMF.[43]

The Executive Board of the IMF had completed 5 out of 12 scheduled reviews under the 3-year IMF-supported program as of June 2020, with the sixth review delayed due to slow progress on the completion of two finance sector prior actions. According to the September 2019 IMF staff report, most structural reforms envisaged at the beginning of the EFF have been implemented.[44] On structural reforms, numerous fiscal, monetary, and financial market reforms have been undertaken since the start of the program. The remaining major structural reform is strengthening the banking sector.

In addition, LCY government bond issuance was temporarily halted by the MOF in October 2017 to reduce government funding costs and drive fiscal consolidation to restore debt sustainability.

2.   Increasing Foreign Investor Interest

Foreign investors have become more active in the Mongolian capital market in recent years, especially in exchange-listed government bond trading and stock trading.

According to the Securities Market Summary of 2018 published by the FRC, foreign investors accounted for 39.2% of the total trading volume of publicly traded securities in 2018, up from just 4.1% in the previous year. In addition, foreign investors formed 7.2% of the secondary market trading volume of government bonds in 2018, compared with 2.8% in 2017.

Because of double-digit interest rates and their tax-free status, LCY government bonds are in high demand from foreign investors and domestic investors alike. Once government bond issuance restarts, foreign investor activity in the Mongolian bond market is expected to grow even further.

---

[43] Footnote 10.
[44] IMF. 2019. IMF Executive Board Concludes 2019 Article IV Consultation with Mongolia. Press Release No. 19/333. 17 September. https://www.imf.org/en/News/Articles/2019/09/17/pr19333-mongolia-imf-executive-board-concludes-2019-article-iv-consultation.

X

Recent Developments and Future Direction

A. Recent Major Developments

This chapter outlines the major recent developments that have had a significant impact on the current state of the overall Mongolian capital market.

1. Capital-Market-Related Legislation Revisions

The Parliament approved the Sustainable Development Vision 2030 with the passage of Resolution No. 19 on 5 February 2016. Under this long-term vision, various national programs are being implemented, including the National Program to Develop the Financial Market until 2025. The Sustainable Development Vision 2030 aims to increase the capital market's share in the finance sector to 10% by 2020 and 16% by 2030, and to decrease the dominance of the banking sector to 90% by 2020 and 82% by 2030.

As part of the Sustainable Development Vision 2030, the Parliament approved the General Directive on Developing the Economy and Society of Mongolia in 2020 by Resolution No. 54 on 30 May 2019. Under the directive, the government is to revise five pieces of legislation related to the capital market, with the goal of creating a legal environment to promote competition and accessibility in the finance sector, increasing product offering, and streamlining regulations. This legislation includes the Securities Market Law and the Company Law, among others. The revisions are expected to remove some of the obstacles for corporate debt instrument issuers and should be completed in 2020 under leadership of the MOF.

2. Revision of Tax Law

The Government of Mongolia approved the National Program to Develop the Financial Market until 2025 with the passage of Resolution No. 299 on 3 October 2017, a program that was prepared under the guidance of the Financial Stability Council of Mongolia by a working group that consisted of the BOM, FRC, and MOF. The program covers various efforts aimed at the capital market, the tax environment of the financial market at large, and other financial sectors. Under the program, tax legislation related to the financial market was revised in March 2019. The revised laws were effective on 1 January 2020.

To support the development of the bond market in Mongolia, the government has been implementing tax exemptions on incomes from bond investments. Although it is only applicable to government bond purchases, the 2019 revision of the tax code allowed for lower taxes on publicly offered corporate bond investments. These tax reductions are applied to both corporate and personal income.

As with the previous laws, income from government bonds and debt securities issued by the Development Bank of Mongolia is tax exempt from corporate and personal income taxes under the revised laws.

However, for corporate debt securities, the following additions have been made in the revised tax laws for the purposes of developing the capital market and reducing commercial bank interest rates:

(i)   Interest income from debt instruments and loans issued by Mongolian commercial banks to domestic and foreign sources are to be taxed 5%.

(ii)   Interest income from debt instruments traded publicly on the domestic and international primary and secondary markets that are issued by a Mongolian taxpaying entity that does not own any exploration and mining licenses for minerals, radioactive minerals, and oil are to be taxed 5%.

(iii) Interest and dividend income from debt instruments, equities, and securities traded publicly on the domestic and international primary and secondary markets that are issued by a Mongolian taxpaying entity are to be taxed 5%.

3.   The International Monetary Fund's Extended Fund Facility

Mining exports constitute up to 90% of the total exports of Mongolia. A sharp drop in commodity prices from 2012 onward severely affected the balance of payments and fiscal position of Mongolia. Macroeconomic policies implemented by the government supported domestic economic growth, but at the cost of increasing public debt, weakening the balance of payments, and reducing banks' asset quality. By the end of 2016, the large fiscal deficit and the depreciation of the currency together pushed general government debt up to nearly 90% of gross domestic product (GDP), according to the IMF.[45]

The IMF press release notes that the Mongolian authorities recognized these economic difficulties and prepared an Economic Recovery Program that would largely reverse past policies. They also approached the IMF for assistance. As a result, the IMF approved a 3-year extended arrangement under the EFF for Mongolia on 24 May 2017 to support the economic reform program along with a USD5.5 billion IMF-led financing package.

The program aims to stabilize the economy, restore confidence, and pave the way to economic recovery. A critical pillar of the program is fiscal consolidation to reduce the pressure on domestic financial markets, stabilize the external position, and restore debt sustainability. The program also lays the foundation for sustainable and inclusive growth in the future. To end the boom–bust cycles of the past, the reform program will (i) discipline fiscal policy; (ii) improve the central bank's independence, governance, and focus on core responsibilities; (iii) strengthen the finance sector; (iv) foster economic diversification and inclusive growth; and (v) protect the most vulnerable in society, according to the IMF press release.

Under the program, many fiscal, monetary, and financial markets reforms have been implemented, with the banking sector structural reform the only remaining major reform. Since 2016, the fiscal balance has improved by 18 percentage points of GDP, public debt declined by 14 percentage points of GDP, and gross foreign reserves roughly tripled, according to the IMF.

---

[45] Footnote 10.

The recovery stems from a stronger policy framework, significant official financing, and a rebound in external demand. Updated information on the IMF program in Mongolia can be found at the IMF website.[46]

4.   Financial Action Task Force Monitored Jurisdictions List

In 2004, Mongolia became a member of the Asia-Pacific Group on Money Laundering (APG),[47] which is closely affiliated with the Financial Action Task Force (FATF), while conducting its operation at the regional level.[48] In addition, Mongolia regularly reports to the APG on its national anti-money laundering and combating the financing of terrorism (AML/CFT) progress and gets an assessment of its operations by the APG. This organization assesses the member countries' level of compliance with the FATF recommendations.[49]

According to the FATF official press releases, in October 2019, Mongolia was added to the FATF list of jurisdictions with strategic AML/CFT deficiencies and made a high-level political commitment to develop an action plan to address these deficiencies.[50] Mongolia was added to the FATF's watch list in 2011 and was removed in 2014 after the country made structural changes to meet some requirements and made specific commitments to meet others. In 2016, the FATF strongly urged Mongolia to enforce the relevant laws with a set of recommendations. The recommendations included enhancing economic transparency, improving oversight of the financial market, and holding those who break laws accountable. Complying with the recommendations, the Government of Mongolia formed the National Council to Combat Money Laundering and Terrorism in April 2017.

However, failing to produce the desired outcomes, despite being under the FATF's enhanced monitoring and making significant progress in addressing the technical compliance deficiencies identified in its mutual evaluation report, Mongolia was added back to the so-called grey list in October 2019.

According to the FATF statement, Mongolia is now committed to implement an additional action plan for enhancing its AML/CFT system, which includes the following:

(i)   improving sectoral money laundering and terrorist financing risk understanding by designated nonfinancial business and professional supervisors, applying a risk-based approach to supervision, and applying proportionate and dissuasive sanctions for breaches of obligations;

(ii)   demonstrating increased investigations and prosecutions of different types of money laundering activities in line with identified risks;

(iii) demonstrating the further seizure and confiscation of falsely or nondeclared currency and applying effective, proportionate, and dissuasive sanctions; and

(iv)   demonstrating cooperation and coordination between authorities to prevent sanctions evasion, and monitoring compliance by financial

---

[46] IMF. Mongolia. https://www.imf.org/en/Countries/MNG.

[47] The APG is the FATF-style regional body for the Asia-Pacific region. It is an intergovernmental organization consisting of 41 member jurisdictions focused on ensuring that its members effectively implement international standards against money laundering, terrorist financing, and proliferation financing related to weapons of mass destruction.

[48] The FATF monitors member countries' progress in implementing the FATF recommendations, reviews money laundering and terrorist financing techniques and countermeasures, and promotes the adoption and implementation of the FATF recommendations globally (its main objectives can be found at FATF. About. What Do We Do. https://www.fatf-gafi.org/about/whatwedo/).

[49] FATF. 2020. *International Standards on Combating Money Laundering and the Financing of Terrorism and Proliferation.* Paris. www.fatf-gafi.org/recommendations.html.

[50] FATF. 2019. Improving Global AML/CFT Compliance: On-going Process. 18 October. https://www.fatf-gafi.org/publications/high-risk-and-other-monitored-jurisdictions/documents/fatf-compliance-october-2019.html.

institutions and designated nonfinancial businesses and professions with their proliferation of financing-related targeted financial sanctions obligations, including the application of proportionate and dissuasive sanctions.

On 23 October 2020, at its plenary meeting, the FATF removed Mongolia from the list of jurisdictions under increased monitoring, citing the progress it made in addressing the strategic AML/CFT deficiencies identified by the FATF in 2019.[51] More recent information on the status of Mongolia with regard to this subject can be found on the FATF website.[52]

5. Introduction of Delivery Versus Payment Settlement

Under the General Directive on Developing Economy and Society of Mongolia in 2020, the FRC introduced delivery versus payment (DVP) settlement into the Mongolian capital market to update the securities settlement system to international standards. Under the FRC Resolution No. 29 of 29 January 2020, Mongolia adopted the DVP with T+2 finality arrangement starting from 31 March 2020.

B. Future Direction

This section reviews some of the planned or expected developments in the legal and regulatory framework in the Mongolian capital market.

1. National Program to Develop the Financial Market until 2025

The government approved the National Program to Develop the Financial Market until 2025, as per Resolution No. 299, dated 3 October 2017. The program was prepared under the guidance of the Financial Stability Council of Mongolia by a working group that consisted of the BOM, FRC, MOF, the Depository Insurance Corporation of Mongolia, and other stakeholders. The program covers the banking industry, insurance sector, capital market, tax environment of financial market, microfinance, market infrastructure, public financial literacy, financial access, savings insurance, and good governance in the financial market.

The program aims to implement the following actions with relation to the capital market:

(i) Revising capital market policy and the regulatory environment, improving regulatory capacity of the regulator, and eliminating duplication of functions:
  (a) stimulate multilateral cooperation with similar foreign regulatory bodies in the field of capital market regulation to study their experiences and cooperate in the creation of a regulatory environment for emerging products, services, and activities in the market;
  (b) draft a revised Law on the Legal Status of the Financial Regulatory Commission to improve the regulatory and monitoring environment for the finance sector;
  (c) transition to a risk-based monitoring system and refine the methods and policies of distance and onsite monitoring, based on the experience of regulatory agencies in other countries;

---

[51] FATF. 2020. Outcomes FATF Plenary. 23 October. http://www.fatf-gafi.org/publications/fatfgeneral/documents/outcomes-fatf-plenary-october-2020.html.

[52] FATF. Mongolia. http://www.fatf-gafi.org/countries/#Mongolia.

(d)   improve market monitoring of securities trading and establish effective electronic monitoring system and integrated database of securities market;

(e)   revise relevant regulations and introduce new regulations to improve the securities market regulatory environment;

(f)   introduce policy support on additional securities issuance, stock split, and mergers of exchange-listed companies, and make amendments to related legislations on establishing maximum limits for holding shares of one company for individuals and legal entities;

(g)   delist in phases the companies that do not meet the requirements of the stock exchange, companies that are suspended from trading, and companies that do not fulfill their legal obligations; update listing requirements to international standards, and take steps to improve the quality of the products traded in the market in conjunction with professional stakeholders;

(h)   improve the regulatory environment by reducing the requirements for companies to issue bonds to develop the primary and secondary markets for corporate bonds;

(i)   create professional investors and special funds to direct financial resources to the capital market;

(j)   improve the quality of products on the market, improve the accountability of companies and improve monitoring by improving the governance, financial reporting, and information disclosure of listed companies;

(k)   introduce new products and services in the capital market, improve financing conditions for small and medium-sized businesses, and create investment incentives; and

(l)   clarify the role of public policy and regulatory bodies participating in the capital market, eliminate duplication, and improve coordination.

(ii)   Policy support to aid increased engagement of market participants:

(a)   examine and resolve the additional requirements for the professional participant organizations stated in the Audit Law and the Asset Valuation Law;

(b)   improve the legal environment and conditions for the operation of rating agencies and support those organizations with policies;

(c)   refine the legal and regulatory framework that ensures the custodian banks' services provide services related to the storage of securities owned by the securities owner and other rights of ownership of the securities, and support their operation;

(d)   improve the regulatory environment to enhance the monitoring system for investment fund and investment management company activities;

(e)   create a favorable environment for investing in a variety of financial instruments by supporting investment funds;

(f)   develop and implement a set of measures to increase the standards and responsibilities of financial reporting, information transparency, and standards of professional participants in the securities market;

(g)   establish requirements for sound financial ratios and solvency indicators of regulated entities in securities market in accordance with international standard, and localize operating standards;

(h)   establish government securities-based derivatives to support the emergence of large professional investors in the domestic market;

(i)   refine the legal framework for the event of bankruptcy and insolvency of regulated securities market participant entities;

(j)   change the regulatory environment to increase the number of regulated entities operating in rural areas;

        (k)   update payment and settlement system in accordance with international standards and transfer to a DVP scheme;

        (l)   create a regulatory environment to promote foreign and domestic investor participation and create a favorable environment for small and medium-sized businesses to attract funding by developing electronic securities trading system; and

        (m)   establish a unified system of settlement among securities exchanges.

    (iii)   Increasing the range of products and services in the industry:

        (a)   create a legal framework for developing and introducing derivative financial instruments to protect against risks;

        (b)   provide policy support for domestic companies to dual list on foreign stock exchanges, issue depository receipts, and companies listed on foreign stock exchanges to dual list their securities on domestic stock exchanges;

        (c)   establish a legal framework for developing and introducing products and services based on new financial technologies;

        (d)   provide policy support to develop a secondary market for asset-backed securities by cooperation among public and policy entities;

        (e)   take step-by-step measures to privatize state-owned enterprises through the MSE;

        (f)   take actions to offer certain percentage of shares of a legal entity holding a strategically important mineral deposit through the MSE;

        (g)   coordinate with government agencies to take appropriate measures to reduce the costs of trading and the number of steps required for market transactions;

        (h)   take measures to provide information to the public and attract public attention to the securities market by distributing and circulating undistributed dividends, shares, and cash balances accumulated at the central depository; and

        (i)   increase market activity and investor participation by providing information and necessary education on market features, products and services, principles of market operation, possible risks, returns, regulatory environment, relation with other sectors, and their impact on the economy.

    (iv)   Maintaining a stable and optimal tax environment for the finance sector:

        (a)   not impose different taxes on activities in the finance sector compared with other sectors and maintain a stable tax environment, and

        (b)   adhere to the same taxation principle on the same financial instruments without distorting financial markets.

In addition, various actions will be taken to improve governance, accountability, and information disclosure in the capital market, as well as systems to combat money laundering and terrorism financing in conformity with international standards.

The program will be implemented in two phases, with Phase I during 2018–2021 and Phase II during 2021–2025. The Financial Stability Council will oversee the program implementation, while the BOM, FRC, and MOF will implement the program. The Steering Committee of the Financial Stability Council will evaluate the program performance semiannually and report to the council. Program performance is to be presented to the Government of Mongolia on an annual basis.

2.   Capital Market Legislative Reforms

In addition to the regulatory reforms being planned under the National Program to Develop the Financial Market until 2025, various legislative reforms related to the capital market are being planned under the General Directive on Developing Economy and Society of Mongolia in 2020, approved by the Parliament as part of the Sustainable Development Vision 2030. As part of these capital market reforms, the government will revise existing legislation—such as the Securities Market Law, the Company Law, and the Bankruptcy Law—to streamline legislation, promote competition and accessibility in the finance sector, and revise the capital market regulations in line with international best practices.

As part of these legislative reforms, clear definitions of default and insolvency provisions are expected to be defined, and the concept of bondholders' representative or bond trustee is expected to be added. In addition, various regulatory obstacles currently faced by corporate debt instrument issuers are expected to be removed to aid the development of the Mongolian bond market.

Moreover, the FRC has been tasked to reduce the number of licenses required to operate in the non-banking finance sector, extend the effective duration of the licenses, and eliminate duplicates in inspections and bureaucratic inefficiencies, as per Article 2.7 of the General Directive on Developing Economy and Society of Mongolia in 2020.

Appendix 1
Group of Thirty Compliance

The Asian Development Bank Secretariat has recently changed its approach for this compliance section to account for other measures in addition to those of the Group of Thirty. An example are the *Principles for Financial Market Infrastructures* defined and monitored by the Bank for International Settlements' Committee on Payments and Market Infrastructures and the International Organization of Securities Commissions.

Background information can be found at Bank for International Settlements and International Organization of Securities Commissions. 2012. *Principles for Financial Market Infrastructures*. April. https://www.iosco.org/library/pubdocs/pdf/IOSCOPD377-PFMI.pdf.

Appendix 2
Practical References

For easy access to further information about the market features described in the Bond Market Guide for Mongolia—including information on the policy bodies, regulatory authorities, and securities market-related institutions—interested parties are encouraged to utilize the following links (most web pages partly available in English):

Bank of Mongolia
https://www.mongolbank.mn/eng/

Financial Regulatory Commission
https://www.frc.mn

Ministry of Finance
https://mof.gov.mn/en/

Mongolian Association of Securities Dealers (only available in Mongolian)
http://masd.mn

Mongolian Central Securities Depository
https://www.schcd.mn/?lang=en

Mongolian Securities Clearing House
http://www.mscc.mn

Mongol Securities Exchange
https://www.msx.mn

Mongolian Stock Exchange
http://mse.mn/en

Mongolian Stock Exchange—Laws
http://mse.mn/en/content/list/167

Mongolian Stock Exchange—Rules and Regulations
http://mse.mn/en/content/list/18

Appendix 3
List of Laws and Regulations

For ease of reference, a list of laws and regulations for the bond and securities market in Mongolia are listed in Tables A3.1 and A3.2, starting with the most recent publication in each category.

Table A3.1: Fundamental or Key Legislation for the Bond Market in Mongolia

Title	Issuer	Issue Date	Effective Date
Debt Management Law	Parliament	18 Feb 2015	18 Feb 2015
Investment Fund Law	Parliament	3 Oct 2013	1 Jan 2014
Securities Market Law	Parliament	24 May 2013	1 Jan 2014
Investment Law	Parliament	3 Oct 2013	1 Nov 2013
Law on Combating Money Laundering and Terrorism Financing	Parliament	31 May 2013	31 May 2013
Company Law	Parliament	6 Oct 2011	21 Nov 2011
Asset-Backed Security Law	Parliament	23 Apr 2010	1 Jan 2011
Law on Settling Payments in National Currency	Parliament	9 Jul 2009	9 Jul 2009
Law on Legal Status of Financial Regulatory Commission	Parliament	17 Nov 2005	17 Nov 2005
Civil Law	Parliament	10 Jan 2002	5 Feb 2002

Source: Adapted by the Asian Development Bank from the official websites of the Parliament, Financial Regulatory Commission, and Mongolia Stock Exchange.

Table A3.2: Key Regulations for the Bond Market in Mongolia

Title	Issuer	Issue Date
Regulation on Primary and Secondary Market Operations of Domestic Government Securities	PM	20 Feb 2019
Regulation on Listing and Reporting of Insider Information	FRC	24 Apr 2019
Regulation on Collateralizing Securities	FRC	26 Dec 2018
Regulation on Securities Market Dispute Settlement Council	FRC	6 Apr 2016
General Procedure for Securities Trading Settlement Activities	FRC	24 Feb 2016
Regulation on Information Transparency of Security Issuers	FRC	17 Dec 2015
Regulation on Securities Registration	FRC	23 Nov 2015
Regulation on Preventing Misuse of the Securities Market	FRC	24 Mar 2015
Regulation on Private Investment Fund Activities	FRC	1 Jan 2015
Regulation on Public Investment Fund Activities	FRC	10 Dec 2014
Regulation on Custodian Licensing and Operations	FRC	3 Jul 2014
Regulation on Registration and Public Offering of Depository Receipts	FRC	25 Jun 2014
Regulation on Insider Information and Regulating Activities of Insider Information Holders on the Securities Market	FRC	15 Jan 2014
Regulation on Operations of Regulated Securities Market Entities	FRC	15 Jan 2014
Regulation on Investment Management Activities and Permits	FRC	15 Jan 2014
Regulation on Regulating Financial Rating Operations	FRC	18 Dec 2013
Regulation on Licensing to Undertake Regulated Activities in The Securities Market	FRC	12 Dec 2013
Regulation on Issuing, Registering, and Licensing of Asset-Backed Securities	FRC	14 Sep 2011
Regulation on Licensing and Registering of Rating Agencies	FRC	24 Mar 2010
Regulation on Remote Monitoring of Securities Issuers	FRC	28 Nov 2008

continued on next page

Table A3.2 continued

Title	Issuer	Issue Date
Regulation on Granting and Inheriting Ownership Rights Certified by Securities	FRC	12 Nov 2007
Primary Market Issuance Rules	MSE	26 Oct 2018
Securities Listing Rules	MSE	25 Jan 2018
Guidelines on Primary Market Issuance of Government Securities	MSE	4 Jul 2017
Guidelines on Submitting Information Electronically for Listed Companies	MSE	28 Apr 2017
Guidelines on Trading Activities	MSE	17 Oct 2014
Trading Rules of the MSE	MSE	10 Feb 2012
Listing Rules of MSX	MSX	24 May 2018
Trading Rules of MSX	MSX	16 May 2018
Rules on Clearing Activities	MSX	16 May 2018
Rules on Monitoring Activities of MSX	MSX	7 Jan 2018
Membership Rules of MASD	MASD	22 Mar 2019
Rules on Conducting Ceremony of Oath for Securities Market Professionals	MASD	10 Mar 2017
Ethical Codes and Professional Standards of MASD	MASD	4 Mar 2016
Rules on Monitoring Member Activities and Resolving Disputes and Complaints	MASD	4 Mar 2016
Rules on Management, Organization and Operation of MASD	MASD	4 Mar 2016
Rules on Conducting Training, Retraining and Issuance of Professional Licenses	MASD	4 Mar 2016
Rules on Preventing Restricted Activities on the Securities Market	MASD	4 Mar 2016
Rules on Registering Ownership Rights Certified by Securities	MCSD	30 Apr 2019
Rules on Securities Depository	MCSD	5 Jul 2016
Rules on Registering Asset-Backed Securities and Registering Ownership Rights in Over-the-Counter Trades	MCSD	5 Jul 2016
Rules on Registering Government Debt Securities	MCSD	5 Jul 2016
Rules on Custodian Membership	MCSD	5 Jul 2016
Rules on Securities Clearing and Settlement of Monetary Assets	MSCH	9 Aug 2016
Rules on Securities Clearing Activities	MSCH	9 Aug 2016

PM = Prime Minister of the Government of Mongolia, FRC = Financial Regulatory Commission, MSE = Mongolian Stock Exchange, MSX = Mongol Securities Exchange, MASD = Mongolian Association of Securities Dealers, MCSD = Mongolian Central Securities Depository, MSCH = Mongolian Securities Clearing House.
Source: Adapted by the Asian Development Bank from the official websites of the FRC, MSE, MASD, MCSD, MSCH, and MSX.

Appendix 4
Glossary of Technical Terms

Open Joint Stock Company	A company whose capital invested by the shareholders is divided into shares, which are listed at an exchange and may be freely traded by the public without regard to preemptive rights of the shareholders (Securities Market Law)
Closed Joint Stock Company	A company whose capital invested by the shareholders is divided into shares, which are registered at the Mongolian Securities Clearing House and Mongolian Central Securities Depository, and which are traded outside of the Mongolian Stock Exchange by means of private subscription (Securities Market Law)
Open Securities	Securities that are offered through public offering or traded publicly on the exchange
Closed Securities	Securities that are offered through private placement or traded privately, and not on the exchange
Public Offering	Offering securities publicly to more than 50 investors under the regulations approved by the Financial Regulatory Commission (Securities Market Law)
Securities Company	"Unet Tsaasnii Company (Securities Company)" or the abbreviation "UTsK," is the name of regulated entities that are required to have a special designation after their company name, except for stock exchanges, legal entities licensed to engage in securities central depository activities, or banks (Securities Market Law)
Debt Instrument	The legal terminology for bond in Mongolian is "debt instrument," as defined in the Securities Market Law and the Company Law
Registration	The term "registration" is used in Mongolia interchangeably among registration, listing, and recording of securities. It is all one word in the Mongolian language.
Securities Clearing	Securities clearing activities shall be understood to be a series of activities carried out in the following order: (i) following a securities trade, determining the payments that the parties which participated in the trade should make in accordance with a contract or agreement on a contract-by-contract and aggregate basis, and making the relevant financial and accounting records; and (ii) preparing trade settlements and issuing payment processing requests to competent settlement institutions (Securities Market Law, Article 43)

Securities Trade Settlement	Securities trade settlement activities shall be understood as a series of activities to be carried out in the following order:

(i)   transferring the payment by the purchaser to the account of the seller in accordance with the instructions of the clearing house;

(ii) depositing the appropriate number of securities that are in the account of the seller of securities into the account of the purchaser;

(iii) performing simultaneous payment transactions by way of issuing instructions to the custodians' central depository and cash depository institutions within the prescribed period;

(iv) making the proper financial records in accordance with the statement of payments, and certifying transactions; and

(v) delivering relevant information to securities depository and registration institutions (Securities Market Law, Article 44)

Securities Central Depository	Securities central depository activities shall mean activities relating to the safekeeping of securities on the basis of a contract entered into with a securities issuer or other participants and maintaining the register in connection therewith (Securities Market Law, Article 45)